6 Coinyie House Close Garden, 7 Fountain Court Garden, 8 Sandeman House Garden, 9 Chessels Court,
10 Moray House, 11 Dunbar's Close Garden, 12 Campbell's Close Garden, 13 Whitefoord House Garden,
14 White Horse Close, 15 The Scottish Parliament, 16 The Palace of Holyroodhouse

Greenyonder Tours is grateful for assistance towards publication from -

The Brownlee Trust
Edinburgh Old Town Association

EDINBURGH WORLD HERITAGE

greatbase
EDINBURGH

Cover photographs
Clockwise, from top left: Chessels Court; Chessels Court; Edinburgh Castle; Dunbar's Close; 17th century garden arch, Moray House; Wild flowers in front of the Scottish Parliament.
Page 7 and page 109 photographs Dunbar's Close.
All above photographs © Jean Bareham.

Hidden Gardens of the Royal Mile

Unexpected green gems in Edinburgh's Old Town

Jean Bareham, Greenyonder Tours

Jean Bareham

27·10·11

First published by Greenyonder Tours, 2011

ISBN 978-0-9570466-0-3

Design by Fiona Menzies
Printed by Stewarts of Edinburgh

Contents

Introduction   11
Greenyonder Tours   12

Part One   Where to find hidden gardens near the Royal Mile   13

Before you go   14
1 The Witches' Fountain, Ramsay Garden and the Outlook Tower   17
2 Johnston Terrace Wildlife Garden   19
3 West Port Garden   23
4 Greyfriars Herb Garden   25
5 Tron Square   28
6 Coinyie House Close Garden   29
7 Fountain Court Garden   31
8 Sandeman House Garden   32
9 Chessels Court   34
10 Moray House   38
11 Dunbar's Close Garden   41
12 Campbell's Close Garden   45
13 Whitefoord House Garden   47
14 White Horse Close   47
15 The Scottish Parliament   49
16 The Palace of Holyroodhouse   53

Part Two   A potted history of people, land and gardens   57

The tree-lined ridge   58
Trading burghs   58
17th Century contrasts   60
Grey Friars, wise women and physic gardens   70
Changing fortunes: 18th, 19th and 20th centuries   76
'Children's gardens in the dark places of the Old Town'   80
20th century - present   91

Part Three   Green shoots   93

A few Old Town gardeners   94
'A small place of nature becomes like the world'   99
Green potential: the Patrick Geddes Gardening Club   103

Select Bibliography   108
Acknowledgements   110
A few organisations of interest   111
Picture credits   112

Holyrood Abbey

Introduction

I like people-watching in Edinburgh's Royal Mile: the melée of visitors jostling up Castlehill and the Lawnmarket to the Castle, stallholders and ghost-hunters milling around St Giles' Cathedral, lawyers striding out to the High Court. Further downhill, in the Canongate, there's more local people just going about their business, and workers, heads down, on their way to offices and shops; there's even the odd just-recognisable MSP and journalist in interview duos around the Scottish Parliament, or a dignitary's limousine purring smoothly into Holyrood Palace.

Probably the last thing most of these people expect to see around the Royal Mile is gardens. Greenery just doesn't fit with the persistent folk memory of dark closes and blackened, looming tenements, nor even the current, livelier reality of street theatre and tartan shops among high, historic buildings.

Yet Edinburgh's Old Town is greening up, and this short guide shows you where to find these hidden green gems. It's designed to be read both 'on the hoof', a practical guide to finding unexpected gardens as you explore the Old Town, and as a longer, satisfying read about the changing fortunes of the Old Town and its gardeners, past and present, that will interest and perhaps even inspire you.

I wish you many happy hours discovering the hidden gardens of Edinburgh's Old Town.

Jean Bareham
Greenyonder Tours

Greenyonder Tours
www.greenyondertours.com

Greenyonder Tours is an Edinburgh-based company offering several short walking tours with the strapline 'See Edinburgh in a Green Light'.

Hidden Gardens of the Royal Mile explores the hidden green nooks and crannies - and grander spaces - of High Street and Canongate.

Green Shoots explores community and wildlife gardening, past and present, around the Castle and Grassmarket, including spaces associated with Scots environmentalist Patrick Geddes. This tour gives you access to the locked Johnston Terrace Wildlife Garden.

Healing Herbs in the City Medical herbalist Julia Cook takes a stroll around the city centre, showing the current medical uses of both familiar weeds and more glamorous garden plants. Also gives you access to the locked Johnston Terrace Wildlife Garden.

Hidden History Royal Botanic Garden Edinburgh guide Jane Corrie takes an unusual route to discover the sites of Edinburgh's old physic gardens, as well as some modern hidden gardens along the way.

Photo opposite: Chessels Court

Part One
Where to find hidden gardens
near the Royal Mile

Before you go

The Royal Mile is the main street in Edinburgh's Old Town, roughly a mile long, from Edinburgh Castle to Holyrood Palace. It has four different street names at different points along its way: from the Castle, running west to east, these are Castlehill, Lawnmarket, High Street, and Canongate.

The gardens can be found just off the Royal Mile, mostly in sheltered closes and courtyards. If you start your explorations from the Castle and walk from west to east, you'll be walking downhill, except of course for some closes, which will involve walking down, then coming back up! Two gardens are slightly further afield, one in West Port near the Grassmarket (3) and another in Greyfriars Kirkyard (4).

The gardens change with the seasons, and all look good from late April to late October. Some look great even in winter, especially those that have a distinct evergreen framework, such as Sandeman House Garden (8), Dunbar's Close (11), and the landscaping around the Scottish Parliament (15). Remember to wrap up warm!

Getting around

Directions Each entry has simple directions, usually from the Royal Mile or, where appropriate, from other points of the Old Town. Using the map (on reverse front cover) along with these directions, you'll be able to find all sixteen gardens and places of interest detailed here.

Accessibility All the gardens, streets and closes are accessible to people of average mobility and fitness, including someone pushing a baby's buggy. For anyone less mobile, each entry has a short description of the terrain involved in walking to and inside the garden, detailing steps, slope and surfaces. Unfortunately, many of the gardens (and the Old Town in general) are either inaccessible or difficult for wheelchair users.

Access Each entry details whether the garden has open access, limited access or is private. Please note where opening hours are given, these are correct at the time of going to print, but may be changed by the authority concerned.

Many of these gardens are in public space, yet are cared for by members of the community, and may have a secluded, even private, 'feel'. Where this is the case, please do visit the garden - it is after all in public space; however, please respect the fact that local residents tend plants and take a pride in these spaces.

Suggested routes

There are various ways you can see the gardens and enjoy the walk:

Simply dip in and out. Visit one or two gardens as you're passing, or take a break from work or shopping and escape to a peaceful oasis. Greyfriars Herb Garden (4), Sandeman House Garden (8), Chessels Court (9), and Dunbar's Close Garden (11) are all good for some restful time out.

You could take in all gardens (1 - 16) in one day: your total distance would be about two miles (given you'll be going off the main road and up and down a few closes). Including time for lingering and enjoying the gardens, you'd want to spend seven to eight hours on the total route.

A gentler way would be to split the route into three visits, for example:

Witches' Fountain (1) to Tron Square (5) Two of the gardens - Johnston Terrace (2) and West Port (3) - are normally closed, but can be glimpsed from the road. The theme here is community, wildlife and herb gardens, and a glimpse back in time into a children's garden of the past. This route is a part of Greenyonder Tours' walking tour 'Green Shoots'. The route is about one mile long and includes going up and down steep steps and slopes, and some cobbled surfaces; otherwise it's mainly pavement walking. Allow about 90 minutes to two hours.

Coinyie House Close (6) to White Horse Close (14) This route closely follows Greenyonder's popular walking tour 'Hidden Gardens of the Royal Mile'. It's approximately one mile of mainly downhill and easy pavement walking, but does include a few steps and steep cobbled surfaces. Allow about two hours.

The Scottish Parliament (15) and the Palace of Holyroodhouse (16) This 'hop and a skip' over the narrow road which divides Parliament and Palace gives a glimpse into the gardens of politicians and royals. It includes booking a free tour of the Parliament building, and taking a paid tour of Holyroodhouse; contact details are given for both. Allow at least three hours.

1 The Witches' Fountain, Ramsay Garden and the Outlook Tower

Detail, Witches' Fountain

Directions The Witches' Fountain is at the east end of the Castle Esplanade. Walk up Castlehill and as soon as you enter the Esplanade, turn right - the fountain is attached to the boundary wall, facing towards the Castle. Once you have seen the fountain, walk down Castlehill the short distance to Ramsay Lane (first left) for Ramsay Garden and the Outlook Tower. Accessibility Uphill pavements and steep cobbled surfaces. Castlehill can be very busy, so to avoid crowds go early in the day. Access The Castle Esplanade is usually open to the public, although access to the fountain may be limited occasionally.

The first three stops by Edinburgh Castle aren't actually gardens, but are all closely linked with pioneer Scots townplanner and environmentalist Patrick Geddes (1856 - 1932) who was to inspire the creation of children's gardens in the Old Town. (more p85) The Witches' Fountain is a stylish Art Nouveau cast iron drinking fountain, designed in 1894 by artist John Duncan, a close friend and collaborator of Patrick Geddes, and erected in 1912, as part of Geddes's mission to encourage public art. The fountain commemorates the 300 women and men executed as witches near this spot between 1492 and the early 1700s. The plants represent the fact that the vast majority of those who suffered this awful death were herbalists and folk healers.

The plaque above reads 'The wicked head and serene head signify that some used their exceptional knowledge for evil purposes while others were misunderstood and wished their kind nothing but good.' All the images seem to represent this dual thinking about those executed for witchcraft: the 'evil eye' on the right side of the square basin is kept at bay by the 'hands of healing' on the left. The foxglove produces poisonous digitalis, yet it is a thing of beauty, and in skilled hands is a healing plant. The leaves to the left of the foxglove are of the Arum lily, a highly poisonous yet deceptively attractive plant, used medicinally in the past as a diuretic and to treat ringworm.[1] On the front of the basin is a winding bindweed - a pernicious weed with a flower as beautiful and delicate as any garden plant.

Ramsay Garden is just on your left, immediately east of the Castle. Commissioned by Geddes in 1892-3, and designed by architects S. Henbest Capper and Sidney Mitchell, the Arts and Crafts-inspired complex of white-harled, timbered, red-tiled buildings incorporates on its north side the earlier home (c1740) of poet Alan Ramsay, known as Ramsay Lodge or Goose Pie House (because of its strangely shaped roof), and a mid-18th century terrace. The complex was part of

Ramsay Garden from the north

Geddes's plan to bring professional families into the area (then a slum). Each flat was designed around the needs of the family who would live in it; Geddes described the fluid design process as an early experiment in 'not house building but home making'.

Today's residents enjoy two private gardens: one is a little locked square, easily visible from the public vantage point of Ramsay Lane. From here you can see the Geddes family's own flat, with the square bay windows and wonderful views all round. The other is a more extensive garden on the northern frontage, which overlooks Princes Street Gardens and has fantastic, clear views over the New Town, the Forth and, on a clear day, over Fife to the Cairngorms; this is also locked, but may be glimpsed through the gate on the left as you go down Ramsay Lane into Mound Place.

On the corner of Ramsay Lane and Castlehill is the Camera Obscura, which Geddes bought in 1892 and renamed The Outlook Tower, recreating it as an innovative educational centre where visitors were invited literally to 'see' Edinburgh within its region and the world. (more p86)

2 Johnston Terrace Wildlife Garden

Directions If approaching from Johnston Terrace, look out for two red telephone kiosks on the south side of the street. Or From the Castle, go down Castle Wynd Steps, cross Johnston Terrace, go down Patrick Geddes Steps (next to two red telephone kiosks). The garden gate is on your right, about half-way down the first flight of steps. Accessibility 25 steps down to the garden from Johnston Terrace. Three steps, and wooden boardwalk within the garden. Access Unfortunately the garden is locked apart from occasional open days; access

Pond, Johnston Terrace Wildlife Garden

can sometimes be arranged by contacting Scottish Wildlife Trust. Or you can visit as part of Greenyonder Tours' walking tours 'Green Shoots' and 'Healing Herbs in the City'.

History The site may have been terraced for a very long time. It's likely that the Iron Age Celts who occupied Castle Rock three thousand years ago would have farmed on these sunny, south-facing slopes. Throughout the medieval period, the kings who made their home in Edinburgh Castle had orchards on the southern and western terraces of Castle Rock. This was the site of Edinburgh's first Gaelic Chapel, built in 1769 for the many Gaelic-speaking soldiers recruited from the Highlands and billeted at the Castle. There were two Geddes gardens very nearby: Castle Wynd just to the southwest and King's Wall just to the east. (more p85)

Plants for wildlife The Scottish Wildlife Trust (SWT) has managed the garden since 1982. Then a neglected wasteland, staff and volunteers gradually cleared the rubbish, planted the trees, laid the hedge and landscaped ponds, a drystane dyke and brick barbecue. The garden has become very important to local wildlife and biodiversity. It attracts frogs, butterflies, hundreds of insects, the odd grey squirrel, and many birds including chaffinch, dunnock, robin, bluetit, songthrush, greenfinch and occasional predator birds like sparrowhawk and grey heron. Local residents see urban foxes making a regular evening visit, as well as rabbits which have become numerous on Castle Rock.

SWT hopes that the garden will inspire town-dwellers to create at least a corner in their gardens that is wildlife-friendly. It's planted to form a variety of habitats -
The birch copse and woodland edge grows native birch, hawthorn, and blackthorn, and non-native buddleia (for butterflies). The hazel and bird cherry trees are coppiced every few years, and the ash trees are pollarded to stop them growing too large and making too much shade.

The wildflower meadow, which includes cowslips, poppies, ox-eye daisies, bluebells and cranesbills, is mowed only once annually, in September, and all the mowings are carefully raked up to keep fertility low (the golden rule of wildflower meadow gardening). If the stock of flowers becomes low, they are replaced with plug plants after mowing. The bumblebee garden where flowering currant, teasel, vipers bugloss, yellow figwort, a self-sown wild rose, all attract bees. Originally planted, these plants are now largely left to their own devices.

The pond was puddled with clay and is home to tadpoles, pond skaters, water boatmen, and the larvae of damselflies and dragonflies. A smaller pond has been left to vegetate naturally to make a boggy patch, frequented by frogs and many insects, and surrounded by yellow irises loved by nectar-feeding insects. Even the wooden boardwalk provides a habitat for the adult frogs who spend their winters underneath it.

The hedgerow of native hawthorn, blackthorn and elder is a favourite place for nesting and feeding birds. The hedge was laid using the traditional technique of splicing the trunks of the young plants which were then laid horizontally so they regenerate with twigs growing upwards. Brush piles, a compost heap and even the drystane dyke provide homes for insects and snails which in turn are food for birds. The ivy on the high south-facing wall provides nesting places for small birds and a home for many insects.

A happy bee

Garden users In the early days, the garden was left open; however, quite serious anti-social behaviour forced SWT reluctantly to close the garden to the general public. They are keen to allow responsible use by groups, schools, local residents, etc. who may apply for access. The garden is enjoyed by all sorts of groups, including local nurseries (more p99), a school for the blind, architectural students on a project, and a counselling service whose clients appreciate a quiet space amongst nature.

A group of volunteers meets once a month to care for the garden. Apart from the bigger jobs of coppicing and tree maintenance, it's now mainly a question of maintaining the balance so that both animal and human users enjoy the space. Paths are kept clear of the encroaching shrubs. Brambles and native hogweed need to be quite ruthlessly kept in check - the birds and insects love them, of course, but they would take over! Nettles make wonderful food for the caterpillars of butterflies and moths; the fact that mammals - including humans - avoid them make the nettle patch a magnet for insects and invertebrates, which in turn attract birds; the nettles are chopped occasionally to encourage fresh leaves. Love your weeds!

3 West Port Garden

Directions From Johnston Terrace Garden, continue down Patrick Geddes Steps, turn right (west) along Grassmarket; cross diagonally to West Port. The garden is at the southwest corner of the Grassmarket, at the bottom of West Port. Accessibility 20 steps and a sloping cobbled surface bring you down from Johnston Terrace Garden to the Grassmarket. Or start from the Grassmarket for flat pavement walking with some cobbled surfaces. Access The garden is locked but as it is terraced, most of the site is visible from the pavement.

History This isn't exactly a 'hidden garden', but is included here as it's the most tangible memory of a Geddes garden. Inspired by the ideas of Patrick Geddes, the garden was one of ten created by the Outlook Tower Open Spaces Committee in the 'dark places' of the early 20th century Old Town slums. (more p85) When the garden was opened in 1910, it occupied a bigger site, with a larger, flat space for games and a seating area, and two walkways which meandered up the slope.

A 1926 Open Spaces leaflet[2] describes it as follows: 'The aim of these gardens is, first, to bring beauty into some of the most dismal and congested areas of Old Edinburgh, where the sun has small opportunity of penetrating with its attendant happiness and health; and second to ensure a place of safety for small children to play out of school hours among growing flowers and trees, and for mothers to rest with their babies in the fresh air, in districts which are more or less out of reach of the public parks.' The leaflet goes on to describe West Port Garden as a very successful venture. A Hut Club House, cleverly built into the terrace wall, was opened in 1924 as a meeting place for girls' and boys' sports clubs and a troupe of Boy Scouts. There was a lot of local support and the garden continued until after World War Two.

Community voices Local residents still refer to this spot as 'the Geddes garden'. For a site of such importance to Edinburgh's 'hidden history', it is now in an unfortunate state, kept tidy by contractors but not cared for as it could be. In spring 2011 six local residents climbed the fence and tidied up, and planted primulas. They have contacted the Council for a key.

One said 'We would love to have shared access to the garden, have benches on the first terrace, and get a tree specialist to prune the trees to allow more light in.' It is hoped that a local school will garden here. The site has great potential as a space for both people and wildlife to enjoy, and as a place to commemorate that great Scots lover of cities, gardens and nature, Patrick Geddes.

Wildlife Last spring, looking into the garden from the pavement, I became aware of a tapping sound; it took me a while to locate its source - then, looking to the ground, just a couple of feet away, I saw a thrush, snail in beak, persistently tapping the shell on a large stone, just like a blacksmith using an anvil; eventually, after several minutes' work, the shell was broken, and the thrush was rewarded with a juicy snail. It was a small reminder that even here, in Edinburgh's 'night-time economy', wildlife will find little green oases like this.

4 Greyfriars Herb Garden

Directions From West Port, walk east along the Grassmarket to the southeast corner, turn right up Candlemaker Row. Enter Greyfriars Kirkyard by the bottom gate on the right if it is open; otherwise, take the main entrance at the top of Candlemaker Row. **Accessibility** From Grassmarket, uphill pavement walking at Candlemaker Row; some cobbled surfaces. Or Flat pavement walking from George IV Bridge; some cobbled surfaces. There are wide paths around the graveyard; some steps which can be avoided. **Access** Greyfriars Kirkyard is open 24 hours a day, 365 days a year.

A herb bed at Greyfriars

History Greyfriars Kirk and Kirkyard have been witness to many important events in Scottish history, including the signing in 1638 of the National Covenant, against the Crown having any right to interfere with the Scottish Church. There are sections of the Flodden Wall in the Kirkyard's west and south boundaries, and parts of the Telfer Wall in the south boundary. And - most famous of all - it was here that Greyfriars Bobby, the Skye terrier, sat for years beside his dead owner's grave.

The herb beds The Kirkyard is well beloved of ghost tours, but there's a much less scary reason to visit. Since 2009, the Grassmarket Community Project has been supporting volunteers to garden here, and to date there are six beautifully planted herb beds, growing over 200 culinary and medicinal herbs, whose uses are recorded on slates within the beds. At the entrance, a wooden sign and small herb bed welcomes you to Greyfriars Herb Garden. If you turn right and take an anti-clockwise stroll around the Kirkyard, you'll encounter the herb beds in this order:

Traditional Medicinal Herb Bed Project gardener Jocelyn Lockhart wanted to celebrate the Grey Friars who had a medicinal garden here from c1447 - 1559, by planting herbs likely to have been used by these sophisticated herbalists. (more p70) Today, the bed includes musk mallow (*Malva moschata* - used for soothing sore throats and skin problems), and bistort or snakeweed (*Polygonum bistorta* - for washing out poison from bites, and helping to stop bleeding when applied to a wound). The large handsome European liquorice plant (*Glycyrrhiza glabra*) was originally brought to the UK by Dominican friars in the 16th century; the dried root can treat colds, coughs and stomach ulcers.

The Kitchen Herb Bed just outside the project's kitchen / café on the far north east corner grows a range of cooking herbs for use by the volunteer cooks, such as sage, oregano, fennel and others, flanked by four towering angelica plants at the corners. Continue walking anti-clockwise to see a larger Culinary Herb Bed with dozens of herbs to spice up your cooking, including lovage, hyssop, chives, and wild strawberry amongst many others.

Near the back of the Kirk, you'll find the Modern Medicinal Herb Bed. Jocelyn says 'We've decided to grow simple, non-poisonous herbs with proven medicinal value, and I'd love people to help themselves, for example, take a few sprigs of feverfew to make a tea if they have a headache.' Walk round the Kirk, passing two 'mort safes', graves covered with a lockable iron structure to deter 18th century body snatchers. Past the Kirk, the Sundial Bed incorporates a wooden arch (made by a woodworking volunteer) and a clever 'sundial' which accurately tells the time if you stand on the stone and 'read' the time according to where your shadow is cast.

Dye bed at Greyfriars

Plants in focus The neighbouring Dye Plants Bed grows dye plants used before the invention of synthetic aniline dyes, and now making a comeback for those who love the softer natural pigments of plant dyes. The bed includes cornflower (*Centaurea cyanus*) whose petals make a blue dye, and dyer's rocket or weld (*Reseda luteola*) whose leaves and flowers have been used for yellow dye since ancient times. In summer there is bronze and green heuchera (*Heuchera sanguinea*), the garden favourite 'Coral Bells', traditionally also called 'alum root' and used as a mordant. Leaves from the handsome and rather trendy-looking black elder (*Sambucus nigra*) give a yellow dye, while boiling the roots with alum produces blue. It's surprising to see a clump of nettles - the tops give an olive-yellow dye - and rhubarb, whose roots yield a pale yellow dye that can be used directly on to cloth, and whose poisonous leaves are used as a natural mordant.

It's interesting to have a collection of dye plants so near the old Dyers' Close, just off Cowgate. Jocelyn hopes that volunteers will use these plants to learn the old craft of dyeing in conjunction with the Grassmarket textiles project.

5 Tron Square

Directions Tron Square is actually made up of two residential squares, built on terraces between the High Street and Cowgate. From Cowgate, enter the (unnamed) passageway directly opposite the junction with Guthrie Street and follow the steps up to the lower Tron Square. Or From the Royal Mile (High Street), go down Old Assembly Close, turn left at the bottom and enter the first Tron Square, turn right and go down 25 steps to the second Tron Square. Accessibility Tron Square is difficult to access for people with impaired mobility. There are 15 steps up from Cowgate. Or From the Royal Mile, Old Assembly Close is a steep, paved downhill slope, then a further 25 steps. Access This is public space with open access.

History Completed in 1900, Tron Square was one of the first municipal housing schemes in Edinburgh, built to re-house people made homeless through slum improvement schemes. The 'deck access' with balconies was designed as a healthier alternative to the tenement stair, and the courtyards gave people some outdoor space. (more p78)

Tron Square was modernised in 1970. The imposing wrought iron clock on the lower square was donated in 1928 by James Farmer Brown, 'a voluntary Christian worker who interested himself in the Cowgate and District'.

Only a minute's walk from the queues at the Edinburgh Fringe Box Office on Old Assembly Close, the little garden is looked after by residents who attended gardening classes held in Coinyie House Close (6) in 2010. It gives lots of summer colour and, as in other sheltered squares off the Royal Mile, is frequented by a surprising number of birds.

6 Coinyie House Close Garden

Directions From Tron Square, go down steps and through the modern block, turn left (east) along the Cowgate, take the fifth left up South Gray's Close. Take second left opening through a metal gate. Or From the Royal Mile (High Street), go down South Gray's Close and, just before the bottom, turn right through a metal gate. **Accessibility** South Gray's Close is a steep cobbled surface; easier from Cowgate. **Access** Coinyie House Close is public space with open access.

Wall mural, Coinyie House Close

History The north side of the court was the site of the old Scots Mint (hence the name 'Coinyie House' from the popular term 'coinie'); the last Scottish coins were minted here in 1709, two years after the Act of Union.

Now a residential courtyard, until 2009 this was a plain space with an overgrown shrubbery that was attracting rough sleepers. For many years, two neighbours looked after literally hundreds of pot plants, arranged round the court. There are two community meeting rooms behind a double red door (just to the right as you enter). In 2009, the Blackfriars Residents Association who meet there secured funding from Edinburgh Council and Edinburgh World Heritage Trust for a garden. A designer helped plan the garden and the hard landscaping was done in the autumn. Over winter, Edinburgh Council provided gardening classes, which were open to all Old Town residents and proved very popular: the result was new friendships and a wee community of (mainly) new gardeners from different areas of the Old Town, eager to garden, and a feeling that things were moving. While most of the garden is cared for communally, there are individual plots where people can choose what they want to grow, now a common practice in community gardening. The planting up was finished in spring 2010.

Autumn hawthorn, Coinyie House Close

To the south of the courtyard is Panmure St Ann's School on the Cowgate, an educational facility for girls with behavioural difficulties. Pupils designed their garden with large planters for fruit trees and herbs, and painted murals which have really brightened up the concreted playground.

Plants in focus Although on a larger scale than most private gardens, the plant choice would be great for a small garden, and many will give colour and interest in the first year of planting, as has been achieved here. The new design includes a formal scented garden of box and lavender, and an 'orchard walk' with ornamental pear trees (*Pyrus calleryana* 'Chanticleer') in new borders. On the west side the long border bed is well-stocked with easy, colourful plants including tulips, foxgloves, lupins and cosmos, with the old stone wall as backdrop. The mature tree on the south west corner (admittedly not a good choice for a small garden!) is a false acacia (*Robinia pseudoacacia*) with its distinctive, craggy, deeply fissured bark. In October, the little tree growing just to the left of the gate as you enter steals the show with glorious autumn colour and bright red berries; it's a hawthorn, *Crataegus laevigata* 'Paul's Scarlet'.

7 Fountain Court Garden

Directions From Coinyie House Close, go back out the gate, turn left, walk up Gray's Close, take last right into Fountain Court. Or From the High Street, enter via Hyndford's Close (next to the Edinburgh Fudge Shop). Accessibility Easier from High Street via Hyndford's Close which is a slightly sloping paved surface. Access Open access to view the garden from the viewing platform; however, please respect the chain and notices indicating 'Private Garden'.

Fountain Court was named for the old street wellhead just to the east, in a wee courtyard off neighbouring Tweeddale Close and marked by an attractive copper statue, encircled by plant names in English, Latin and Gaelic. Fountain Court now accommodates a sheltered housing complex built by Castlerock Housing Association in the 1980s. The terraced garden was developed at the same time, making it probably the earliest Old Town community garden. It's looked after by the housing association and several residents. Given its sheltered south-facing position, bedding plants can flower right through the winter.

Plants in focus The tree is a Swedish whitebeam (*Sorbus x intermedia*), a good plant for surviving traffic pollution. Like the native whitebeam (*Sorbus aria*) grown in Dunbar's Close (11), the leaves have a fresh, grey-green, slightly furry-looking underside, and there are juicy red berries in autumn which are much loved by birds. This specimen fits the site really well; however, residents feel that if it gets any bigger they may ask for it to be lopped a bit.

8 Sandeman House Garden

Directions From the High Street, enter via Trunk's Close; the opening is almost opposite the entrance to Fountain Court (Hyndford's Close), and just west of John Knox House and the Scottish Storytelling Centre. Accessibility Trunk's Close is a steep paved surface. There are

Sandeman House Garden

steps within the garden. Access The garden is open to the public during office hours - approximately 9.30 am - 5.00 pm on weekdays only.

As you walk down Trunks Close, the building to your right is Mowbray House, built c1597, and now the oldest inhabited building in Edinburgh. Almost at the bottom of the close, turn right, and the garden opens up before you. The old stone archway on your right used to lead into the old Hope's Close.

History Sandeman House was built in the

19th century by the Free Church of Scotland and is named after Reverend John Sandeman who did missionary work in the area. Scottish Book Trust are tenants of the building, and caretakers of the garden. The building's owners, landscape architects Turnbull Jeffrey Partnership renovated and re-designed the garden in 1996 in a joint initiative with Lothian and Edinburgh Enterprise Ltd (LEEL), then a public body.

The design is stunning and creates a completely different 'feel' to what had been a fairly nondescript piece of land. It's

A bookish cockerel, Sandeman House Garden

surprising, too: the circular motif, repeated throughout the garden, is unusual in the Old Town, which is still laid out in the medieval grid pattern; the space is sometimes used for storytelling 'in the round' and won an award in 2000 for environmental design. The cockerel was made by Phil Johnson of Ratho Byres Forge (seven miles west of Edinburgh) using unpolished stainless steel.

Plants in focus Facing north, and surrounded by buildings, the sun doesn't reach the garden for much of the year, and it's a great place to come for ideas for planting up shady areas. The planting is clever and sophisticated, there is something of interest all year round, and yet the plants are mainly unfussy and easy to grow. Across from the viewing platform, three *Viburnum plicatum tomentosum* 'Mariesii' (called the 'wedding cake bush' because of its habit of growing in 'tiers') have an abundance of white flowers in spring and good autumn colour. Easygoing cranesbills (the mainly native *Geranium*) flower in summer. Behind the cockerel, pollarded acers give a French feel to the garden and have fabulous autumn colour. The low-growing *Epimedium x rubrum*, planted at the front of the main bed left of the cockerel, is a classy plant giving almost all-year-round colour and interest.

The shrubby tree next to the viewing platform is *Davidia Involucrata*, the 'pocket handkerchief' or 'dove' tree, named for the slightly ghostly white bracts, hanging below clusters of tiny flowers in June. This is a case of planting for the future: to date, this specimen hasn't flowered, but gives great autumn colour. Rowan trees behind have grown tall, reaching for the light - probably deliberately, to give a feathery curtain when viewed from the Storytelling Centre window; flowers and berries appear on the top branches, and are better seen from the window.

The large mature tree opposite the main viewing platform is a Southern Beech *(Nothofagus obliqua)*, a native of the Southern Hemisphere. I've been told by one of the original landscapers that this huge tree was brought into this awkward space by 'six burly men, a crane and much bad language!'

9 Chessels Court

Directions There are several entrances to Chessels Court from the Royal Mile (Canongate), including through the arcade just west of the Canons' Gait pub, 232 Canongate. Accessibility There are no steps when you enter via the arcade. There are a few steps to one of the gardens. Access Chessels Court is public space with open access.

History Today, its little community gardens, airy square, and glimpses of private gardens, makes Chessels Court well worth a visit on a 'hidden gardens' tour. Yet it has a chequered history. The middle section of Chessels Buildings on the south of the court was built in the 1740s by property developer Archibald Chesils who sold the flats as 'gentlemen's mansionhouse apartments'; he added the east and west wings in the 1760s. (more p78) From the 19th - mid-20th century, the Court was built up and became very overcrowded. From 1908-77, Saint

Entrance to Chessels Court

Saviours Child Garden Nursery was housed in the ground floor flat, and, as today, enjoyed the private garden to the rear: as one of the Old Town's 'child gardens' offering free childcare for poor children, the children were encouraged to garden, keep pets and spend much of the day outdoors. (more p80) There was a 'Geddes garden' in part of the courtyard from 1912 - c1930. (more p85) The Court was extensively restored in the 1960s. The central courtyard was raised, using the rubble from demolished Victorian tenements (a decision which more recently may have saved the Court from becoming a carpark!).

From the arcade entrance off Canongate, walk clockwise round the Court and you'll see these gardens:

The courtyard The Council look after the grass and trees; all the other plants are looked after by several keen gardener residents. In early spring 2009 the courtyard was carpeted with the delicate pink wildflower lady's smock; the Council left the grass to grow to allow them to regenerate; in subsequent years there have been a few.

Jardins Publics Garden (southeast corner) In 2007, a project called 'Jardins Publics' which was a part of the Edinburgh International Festival worked with the Residents Association to make a garden here. At the end of the Festival, the residents were able to buy the design and plants for the nominal sum of £1. A few residents now look after the garden, and others snip the herbs for cooking.

Gated private garden In 2004, three of the residents decided to make a drab passageway into a garden. When digging the borders, they unearthed lots of oyster shells, a common food in the Old Town for centuries (and now an endangered species!). The spot is so sheltered, they are growing a palm.

Private bed (left-hand gable extension) This is one of the cleverest plantings in the whole tour: the flat-owner gardens on a tiny strip of soil, yet he is supporting at least five climbers that give interest at

Climbers, Chessels Court

different times of the year. There are two clematis (spring and summer), white jasmine and golden hop (summer and autumn) and *Garrya eliptica* (winter 'tassels' and evergreen foliage). Note the heart-shaped ivy on the adjacent wall, which, like all these climbers, is kept in crisp shape with regular pruning.

Private garden, Chessels Court

In front of the opposite gable extension, barrels have recently been planted up with rhubarb and a variety of shrubs and annuals. The beds in the cobbled surface on the west side of the Court look wonderful in summer with annuals and even some red chard.

Plants in focus Residents are proud of the large willow tree in the courtyard; in fact, the Chessels Court Residents Association have a sketch of it as their logo. The willow theme is taken up in the Jardins Publics garden, where there are three miniature willows. There's *Salix pekinensis* 'Tortuosa', a contorted willow with its noticeably twisted twigs and distorted leaves. In the middle bed you'll see the small, weeping Kilmarnock willow (*Salix caprea* 'Kilmarnock'); this dwarf variety of the pussy willow was found growing wild in Scotland and has since become popular in gardens as a trained or grafted standard. The third willow is one so small that at first I didn't believe it was a willow at all: the Flamingo willow (*Salix integra* 'Flamingo') is a Japanese plant with white and pink-tinged foliage. Luckily, these three don't share the problem, associated with larger willows, of creeping roots which can damage the foundations of buildings, although the contorted willow is fast-growing and needs pruning to keep it within bounds.

10 Moray House

Directions From Canongate, turn into St John Street; ignore the main entrance on your left, and use the next entrance, through a smaller gate; the building just in front of you (now the campus reception) is the old nursery. Accessibility St John Street involves pavement walking with a slight slope. Viewing the stone arch involves six steps (or you can view from St John Street). Access This is University of Edinburgh property, with public access to campus grounds on weekdays for most of the year. If closed, you can view some of the features from St John Street. The original Moray House building is normally closed to the public except for occasional openings such as Doors Open Day in September.

17th century gate, Moray House

The building Moray House was built c1625 for the Dowager Countess of Home, one of a number of aristocrats attracted over the 17th to 18th centuries by the Canongate's available land for large townhouses and gardens. Before turning off Canongate, see the old Moray House where it fronts on to the street, with its corbelled balcony and the old wrought iron gate (currently chained) with unusual, sharply pointed ashlar gateposts. The back of the house can be viewed from the central campus carpark. Moray House is a Grade 'A' listed building, and a fine example of a 17th century Scots aristocratic townhouse; I find the building reserved on the outside, yet inside, with its beautiful timberwork, plasterwork and painted ceilings, it is quite exuberant (perhaps like the Scots ourselves!) None of the current campus buildings would have existed in the 17th and 18th centuries, and from here, the house would enjoy clear views south over the garden and Salisbury Crags.

The 17th century garden The extent of the 17th century garden can be seen on the Rothiemay map of 1647. (reverse back cover) Lady Home created a stunning, south-facing, formal walled garden, which, with its extensive orchard, was for many years regarded as the most beautiful in the Canongate. It was laid out in three or four terraces, linked by elegant stone staircases. (more p62) Only two features of the 17th century garden are still visible: the first is a Renaissance gateway of polished ashlar, which you can see by going down the few steps in front of the nursery building and turning left. The gateway, with its elaborate pediment, dates from the 1620s and was originally part of the boundary on to what is now Holyrood Road; the cast iron gate is of a later period.

The second is a small, pantiled summerhouse located at the south east corner of the campus; to see it, walk down St John Street, turn left to walk along Holyrood Road until you are at the end of the campus: the summer house (or a part of it) can be seen through gates, looking like a humble lean-to against a 19th century brewery wall; look more closely, however, and the craftsmanship of the round-arched windows and doors becomes clear. Legend has it that the summerhouse was the location (or one of several locations) for the signing of the Act of Union which united the Scottish and English Parliaments in 1707. The Act was very unpopular locally, and there is documentary evidence that signatories were chased over Canongate garden walls and through shrubberies, so there may be some truth in the legend!

The nursery Moray House, now the University of Edinburgh's School of Education, opened as a teacher training college in 1848. The nursery building (now the campus reception) was built in 1932 as a purpose-built demonstration nursery where student teachers would observe children at play (there are some charming hand-written essays on show in the little museum within the reception building which you can access during office hours). Designed on the educational principle of 'letting the outdoors in', the wall-length glass doors open in concertina fashion, allowing almost no barrier between inside and out. Old photographs show children running out to a front garden in all seasons, and sleeping on the verandah.

Plants in focus While the main reason for visiting Moray House is to imagine its grand garden 'hidden' in the past, there are some very fine plants in the border in front of the nursery, planted up in 1998 to celebrate 150 years as a teacher training college. To the left and right of the steps in front of the nursery, the large shrub rose *Rosa xanthina* 'Canary Bird' enjoys having room to spread out its long, arching stems; if you visit in May, you'll be treated to the sight of these large shrubs covered in single yellow roses. Walk towards the carpark, and beside the steps to Paterson's Building, a pale pink rock rose (one of the *Cistus* family) scrambles down the wall and is exuberant in summer. The plant is a sub-shrub from the Mediterranean and likes very light soil with plenty of drainage and lots of sun: qualities that are not always available in Edinburgh.

On the way As you walk down Canongate to Dunbar's Close garden, you'll pass Acheson House on the right (just east of the Museum of Edinburgh, set back from the street with a little courtyard in front) and, opposite on the left, Canongate Kirkyard. In summer 2011, the Patrick Geddes Gardening Club was given permission to garden in both of these sites. (more p103)

11 Dunbar's Close Garden

Directions Walking downhill (east) along Canongate, Dunbar's Close is the first close on the left after Canongate Kirk. Accessibility Canongate is moderately easy pavement walking with a slight downhill slope. Cobbled surface at entrance to the garden; within the garden there are two flights of about six steps each. Access As a City of Edinburgh park, the garden should be open to the public 7 days per week every day except Christmas and New Year's Day. Winter: approximately 9am - 4pm. Summer: approximately 9am - 6pm.

Burns Monument from Dunbar's Close Garden

History This beautiful and peaceful garden is designed to celebrate the Canongate gardens of the 17th century. Yet it was started in the mid-1970s, on a gap site covered with rank weeds. The land (three-quarters of an acre) became available when a tenement was demolished and was bought by the Mushroom Trust, a private charitable trust interested in promoting green spaces around Edinburgh, with the far-sighted intention of making a public garden. What you see today is not intended to be an exact restoration of anything that might have been on this site, rather it aims to capture the spirit of those large, formal Canongate gardens. (more p61) The Close is probably named after David Dunbar, Writer to the Signet who owned the tenements at the entrance.

The Trust commissioned Seamus Filor to design the garden, taking his inspiration from the formal style depicted in Rothiemay's map. This style admirably suits the Scottish climate: Canongate Kirkyard's high stone wall protects the garden from the west, and elsewhere Filor has created little sheltered 'rooms' by planting high evergreen hedges (mainly yew). Filor then researched the plants. With a few exceptions, the plants here are modern varieties of plants grown in 17th century Scotland. One departure was a decision not to grow vegetables; gardens of the period were always productive, and would certainly have grown vegetables and medicinal and culinary herbs. However, there are fruit trees here, and a fair few herbs, including chives, fennel, rosemary and lavender.

When the garden was completed in 1977, it was gifted to the City of Edinburgh, and is now run by the Parks Department. However the Mushroom Trust continues to support the garden, by employing a gardener and a garden adviser who liaises between the Trust and the Council.

Entrance or first parterre[3] The plaque on the left hand wall as you enter is by stonecarver Gillian Forbes, who also carved some of the inscriptions on the Scottish Parliament's Canongate Wall. Most of the hedging and balls are box, while the central ball of each square is yew. The tree in the centre is a tulip tree (*Liriodendron tulipifera*) which was planted in 1990, and

The long border, Dunbar's Close Garden

Round and about Looking north over the garden, especially in winter, you catch nicely framed views of the Doric colonnades of the former Royal High School (1825) up on Calton Hill. On the left, the round tower in the shape of a telescope is the Nelson Monument (1807), and on the right is the (Robert) Burns Monument (1830). As you walk round the garden, the building opposite the long border is the old stable block, now converted into homes which share the private garden in front. Looking over the private garden, you have a clear view of Panmure House, built c1691 for the Earls of Panmure, one of whom is thought to have introduced the laburnum to Scotland. The Enlightenment economist Adam Smith lived here from 1772 until his death in 1790. To the right is the 18th century Cadell House.

12 Campbell's Close Garden

Directions From Canongate, walking east, turn left into Campbell's Close (just next to Clarinda's tearoom), go down the steps. Accessibility Canongate has a slight downhill slope; moderately easy pavement walking. Two flights of six and three steps at entrance to the garden. Access Open access; please close the gate after your visit.

This new garden was laid out in spring 2010, and is a great improvement on the

Sunny corner, Campbell's Close Garden

previous rather drab grass. The improvements were funded by Edinburgh Council who still look after the grass; the plots of flowers and vegetables are looked after by several residents who joined in with the Coinyie House garden classes in 2010. They got permission to have one of two mature sycamores cut down, as well as an overgrown border of straggly conifers, and the result is a much lighter space. The paintings on the wall are the work of local artist Myer Lacome.

Wildlife To date, slugs seem not to have discovered this newly cultivated space! However, when they do (as inevitably they will), it's hoped that some of their predators will be around, attracted by the sycamore log pile, constructed to invite in insects which in turn attract birds. Unfortunately, the hope of attracting hedgehogs has so far met with no success. Hedgehogs, whose numbers are in decline anyway, are more likely to patronise lush suburban gardens than the tarmac, steps and traffic of the Old Town. However, they were once here: the first garden made by Lileen Hardy was in fact in the neighbouring Brown's Close (more p82). In *Diary of a Free Kindergarten*, in her entry for June 1908, Miss Hardy reports much excitement caused by 'a hedgehog on a week's visit'!

Wall art, Campbell's Close Garden

Round and about The flats looking on to the Canongate were designed by Basil Spence. The flats to the north of the garden are converted from an old independent brewery, as is the block across Calton Road.

13 Whitefoord House Garden

Directions From Campbell's Close Garden, continue down Campbell's Close; when you reach the end, turn right on to Calton Road, and the back gates to Whitefoord House are just there. Accessibility Campbell's Close has a moderately steep slope with cobbled surface. Access Whitefoord House grounds are private land, closed to the public. The garden can be viewed only through the gate.

The large white house is Whitefoord House, built in 1766, and now a housing association for veterans of the armed services. The garden is cared for by a professional gardener. Although closed, it is worth having a 'peek' through the gates on Calton Road as this garden, with its clipped lawn and carefully pruned modern roses, has a different style from the others off the Royal Mile. Every year, there's a day in mid-June when I turn that corner and the roses have all burst into highly colourful bloom since my last visit.

14 White Horse Close

Directions White Horse Close is the last close on the right as you walk down Calton Road, accessible via a narrow set of steps. Or From Canongate, it is the last close on the left as you walk down. Accessibility Calton Road has cobbled surfaces (pavement on the left of the road); access to White Horse Close involves three steps and short, sloping paved surface. Access from Canongate is easier, with paved surfaces and no steps. Access Public space with open access.

History It is fun to enter the close from Calton Road via the narrow steps, as there's a

The old White Horse Inn

sense of anticipation until the courtyard opens out in front of you. Before leaving Calton Road, notice to your left the handsome arched doors, which were the stable doors at the back of the old White Horse Inn. Built in the 17th century, the Close was first the royal mews, then a coaching station for coaches travelling between Edinburgh and London, a busy place in its day, with a well (still visible near the Canongate entrance) and blacksmith's forge as well as the Inn and stables.

By the early 20th century, White Horse Close had fallen into disrepair, and was the first of the Council restorations in the 1960s. The dates 1623 and 1962 are carved into the Inn facade. The architects, Sir Frank Mears and Partners wished to create an 'outdoor community' and to some extent have succeeded: children still play here (which unfortunately is not the case with all closes) and neighbours do sit out to have a chat.

Plants in focus Today, its picturesque houses, pantiled roofs, stepped gables and colourful plants makes White Horse Close one of the favourite spots on the 'Hidden Gardens' tour. I love the way that each household has a garden in pots, and each has their own style. One household has gone productive, with containers brimming with lettuces and potatoes as well as a spectacular fuchsia. Another has gone creative, with home-made pots with 'picket fences' on top to contain the flowering plants within. And everyone's favourite: old-fashioned lacing shoes make containers for sempervirens (extremely hardy plants which look a bit like cactus) in winter and nasturtiums in summer.

Old shoe containers, White Horse Close

15 The Scottish Parliament

Directions The Scottish Parliament is on Horse Wynd, at the very bottom of the Canongate. To follow the gardens and landscaping as described here, begin at Reid's Close, which is the last close on the right as you walk down Canongate. Accessibility Moderately easy pavement walking, with a slight slope. The Parliament building is fully accessible. However, if you have any doubts, please contact the Parliament's Visitors Service directly. Access Reid's Close and the landscaping around the Parliament are open public space. The Parliament Garden is closed to the public; however, if you book a free guided tour, you'll be taken to the Garden Lobby, from where you get a good view of the garden. For details of opening hours, and to book a free guided tour, contact the Scottish Parliament directly. www.scottishparliament.uk tel: 0131 348 5200 or 0800 092 7600

History The first Scottish Parliament for nearly 300 years opened for business in May 1999, and was housed in temporary accommodation until the new building opened in October 2004. The Parliament is built on the site of a Scottish and Newcastle Brewery.

A walk around the Parliament grounds Start at Reid's Close, the last close on the right as you walk down the Canongate. Just as you enter Reid's Close, on your left you'll see a private backgreen, with its very attractive 'Parliament' planting. I have always been fascinated by the fact that this 'ordinary' backgreen, still used by flat-owners here, is enclosed by the high Parliament fence. Continuing down the Close, the Bamboo Garden runs alongside the MSP Building on the left and provides green relief from the hard building materials. As you walk down the Close, with its paving of granite sets, you have a first view of Salisbury Crags.

Go back onto Canongate, turn right, passing the gated entrance to Queensberry House on your right on the way down. Part of the brief to the architect Enric Miralles was that the Parliament building should absorb this 17th century mansion, built c1667, and bought by the first Duke of Queensberry in 1689. An archaeological excavation undertaken from 1998 - 99, just before building work began on the Parliament site, found deep soils of a medieval date on the south side of Queensberry House, confirming there had been a functional backland in the medieval period. (more p59) There was ample evidence too of a formal garden from the late 17th century onwards. (more p61) The garden seems to have had two significant make-overs over the next

Rowan tree on Reid's Close

hundred years or so, presumably reflecting changing tastes and fashions. The first garden was developed c1679 as a typical aristocratic Canongate garden of formal, compartmentalised beds, probably on three terraces linked by stone staircases. Around 1750, the terraces were infilled, creating a large single, sloping garden, rather than individual beds. Around the end of the 18th century, a formal garden featured a parterre arrangement on completely flat ground (so flat, in fact, that it was later made into an army parade ground).

Just past Queensberry House, the Canongate Wall begins. Forming the Parliament boundary, the overall design of the wall was by Sora Smithson and contains a range of 26 stones, from different regions of Scotland, set into large pre-cast concrete panels. Each stone is carved with a quotation to illuminate Scotland or the Parliament, and several refer to plants and nature; my own favourite is:

> What would the world be, once bereft
> Of wet and wildness? Let them be left
> O let them be left, wildness and wet;
> Long live the weeds and wilderness yet.
>
> Gerard Manley Hopkins (1844 - 99), *Inversnaid*

At the lower end of the wall is a townscape based on a sketch of the Old Town by Enric Miralles. Continue down: once you turn right towards the entrance to the Parliament, the landscape just takes over. This is Arthur's Seat and Salisbury Crags, one of Edinburgh's great views, which was opened up when the Parliament replaced the old brewery, whose boundary wall went all the way to the roadside.

The landscaping in front and to the south of the Parliament is public space, well-used by politicians, journalists, and for regular demonstrations, but mainly as a place for meeting friends, a sandwich or a stroll; it is also at times a skateboarder's paradise! Architect Enric Miralles spoke of the Parliament 'sitting in the land'. The landscaping is a mixture of fairly traditional cut turf and a more informal area; there are three ponds in front of the Parliament entrance, which reflect the sky and hillside. There is a story that Miralles took a walk up Arthur's Seat one morning to collect wild plants (actually an illegal act!) which he then strewed on the boardroom table, saying that this was the planting he wanted for the less formal landscaping. All year round, these indigenous wild plants draw the eye naturally up the slopes of Arthur's Seat, with flowers in spring and summer, followed by seedheads in autumn. (Unfortunately, many of these wild plants failed in summer 2011, so let's hope this is tackled for future years.)

The oak and lime trees in the landscaped area were planted to mirror those around the perimeter of Holyrood Palace. There are several single rowan trees in various locations around the Parliament, including one planted near the public entrance. Rowans traditionally symbolise protection.

The leaf motif Miralles used leaf shapes throughout the building and landscaping to symbolise Scotland's land, including the leaf-shaped canopy over the entrance: stand under this and look up to see leaf shapes cut out of the canopy. If you arrange a tour of the building, you'll visit the Garden Lobby. With its twelve leaf-shaped roof lights, this internal space is located on the south side of Queensberry House, and designed as a light and open informal meeting place for MSPs, staff, media and visitors; it is often the setting for televised interviews with politicians. The Parliament Garden (not accessible to the public) is based on a Scottish knot garden, with low box hedges, a small herb garden growing marjoram, lavender, rosemary, thyme, and sage, and a trellis supporting apple and pear trees, planted as a reminder that the garden is located on the site of the 17th century Queensberry House orchard. With a bit of imagination, the view from the Garden Lobby windows over the Parliament Garden somehow 'feels' like the view a 17th century visitor might have had of the Earl of Queensberry's terraces.

Leaf shapes in the Garden Lobby

16 The Palace of Holyroodhouse

Directions The entrance is on Horse Wynd, directly opposite the Scottish Parliament. Accessibility The gardens are accessible. The public rooms in the Palace are largely accessible, except for two small rooms associated with Mary Queen of Scots, which are up a narrow staircase. Please discuss any worries about accessibility with Palace staff. Access The Palace is the Queen's official residence in Scotland, open to the public throughout the year, except when members of the Royal family are in residence. The gardens may be included as part of a visit from 1 April to 31 October; a short garden tour (included within the admission charge, recurring several times daily) was introduced in summer 2011, and may be repeated in future years. Charges apply. www.royalcollection.org.uk tel: 0131 556 5100

History Holyrood Abbey was founded by King David I in 1128; surrounded by royal hunting grounds, the Abbey had lodgings for royal visitors over several centuries. By the 15th century, royals were choosing to spend time at Holyrood Abbey, with its parkland and spacious gardens and orchards, in preference to windy Edinburgh Castle. In 1503, James IV cleared the ground close to the Abbey and built a palace for himself and his bride, Margaret Tudor. Their son, James V also undertook major new building work; however, much of this was later destroyed by fire. The modern

Holyrood Abbey ruins

Palace is the result of the rebuilding of 1671-6 under Charles II, demonstrating architect William Bruce's skill in synthesising old and new; the baroque interiors and the building itself put Holyroodhouse at the forefront of fashion of the time.

The gardens also have a chequered history. In the early days, marshy ground at the foot of Arthur's Seat was drained, enclosed within a wall and cultivated as a monastic garden. For nearly four centuries, the Abbey gardens were primarily under monastic control, until James IV claimed most of the grounds for his palace. By the time his granddaughter Mary Queen of Scots was in residence, there was a series of enclosed gardens, including a walled privy garden, and areas for recreation including jousting, archery, and a tennis court. The two surviving relics of these gardens are Queen Mary's Bath, probably a 16th century garden building, and a faceted sundial (1633), which can now be seen in the north garden. The privy garden was removed in Queen Victoria's time when a new carriage drive was laid to the north avoiding the Canongate slums. Trees were planted to screen nearby gasworks and breweries.

The garden today The ten-acre gardens incorporate the Abbey ruins which date from c1195 - 1230. The most ingenious feature of the garden's Victorian design is the way the boundary wall to the southeast is made invisible by a sloping grassy bank, recently planted with fruit trees, thus concealing the boundaries and giving the impression that the gardens flow into the natural landscape of Holyrood Park. (The boundary, seen from outside the Palace grounds, is actually a ten foot wall.) Wild areas, including an attractive area of wild grasses and cranesbills next to the

The Fiddler, Palace of Holyroodhouse Garden

Abbey ruins, attract owls, woodpeckers, bats, foxes, squirrels and even stoats. There are some quirky features, like the 19th century statue by Robert Forrest called 'The Fiddler', with its worn soft sandstone features. Queen Victoria didn't like it much, and had it hidden away!

Plants in focus The long Jubilee Border, with the Crags as a backdrop, was planted with a

silver and blue theme for the Queen's Silver Jubilee in 1977, then largely replanted for the Golden Jubilee in 2002 with a golden theme, including yellow roses, coreopsis, potentillas and verbascum; these combine well with some of the remaining blue and silver plants including large ornamental thistles, the lavender blue spires and silver foliage of Russian sage (*Perovskia* 'Blue spire') and Lamb's ears (*Stachys byzantina*). The planting is at its best during Royal Week around end of June, when the Queen is in residence and the annual garden party for up to 7,000 guests takes place. A new planting scheme is planned for the Queen's Diamond Jubilee in 2012.

Photo opposite: The first Free Kindergarten, Reid's Court

Part Two
A potted history of people, land and gardens

The tree-lined ridge

The human story of the area we now call Edinburgh's Old Town has always been determined and constrained by its geology and geography. 350 million years ago, long before human beings, Arthur's Seat and Castle Rock were neighbouring volcanoes, situated around the Equator. Over millennia, as the land mass around them inched northwards, their vast bulk was worn away to the small bumps they are now. Much later, during the Ice Age 20,000 years ago, huge glaciers advanced from the west, forcing their way round Castle Rock, gouging out the sandstone valleys we now call the Grassmarket and Princes Street Gardens, and creating between them the distinctive spine on which the Royal Mile now stands.

People have been living and cultivating in this area for at least 3,000 years, perhaps longer. Flint tools used by Bronze Age hunters have been found around Holyrood. Late Bronze Age people built a fortified settlement on Arthur's Seat, where today there remains clear evidence of ancient terracing. Looking west, these Celtic farmers would have looked down on a mile-long, rock-strewn ridge, native trees growing out of its sandstone-based soil. They'd know there was good hunting and fishing in the valleys on either side of the ridge, later to become Holyrood and Calton Roads, with their streams and marshland meeting to make a boggy loch around Holyrood. They'd be in close contact with their neighbours who occupied another, smaller settlement at the ridge's western extremity, on Din Eidyn, now Castle Rock, where there has been a fortified settlement for 3,000 years.

Trading burghs

By the 12th century, much of the land on the south and west slopes of Castle Rock and beyond was given over to royal parkland, orchards and gardens to feed and amuse the court at the Castle (although Edinburgh did not become the capital until the 15th century). Monastic gardens took advantage of the sunny southern slopes of the ridge, at St Giles, and the Black Friars' garden, sited around the area of the present Infirmary Street and Cowgate, as well as at Holyrood Abbey. A street was emerging along the 'spine', from Castle to Abbey.

The Royal Mile as we know it began at this time too, when King David I encouraged wealthy merchants to settle as 'burgesses' in the royal burghs of Edinburgh (founded c1124 - 27) and Canongate (1140), enjoying special rights and privileges to govern themselves and to support trade within their boundaries. People from the surrounding countryside were given permission to come into town to sell produce and goods, and to buy iron and salt, while the burgesses brought in goods from all over Europe.

The merchants - Flemish, Norman, English and Scandinavian as well as native - were given rectangular plots of land set out along both sides of the main street, with the King's consent to build a house on the 'foreland'. In the early days, when there was less pressure for space, each 'backland' would feed a household: there they would keep livestock and grow vegetables such as leeks, fat hen and syboes (spring onions). Some had barns and 'doocots', providing a supply of pigeons as a delicacy. To supplement this, 'indwellers' - those living in the burgh without burgesses' privileges - might venture outside the town to collect fungi and wild berries; archaeological evidence in other towns point to the consumption of brambles, blaeberries, raspberries, wild cherries, rowans and elderberries.[4]

At the bottom of each backland was a well - still causing problems for engineers today. Officials called linesmen ensured the boundaries were kept. Eventually, as the population grew, backlands became divided, public access was needed and the passageways between the lands became known as 'closes'. Walking along the Royal Mile today, you'll see the herringbone pattern formed by many of these same medieval closes. (Edinburgh and Canongate remained separate burghs, technically until the incorporation of the Canongate into the City of Edinburgh in 1856.)

17th Century contrasts

Five centuries later, the Rothiemay map of 1647 (see map 2) tells a fascinating graphic story about the different ways the two burghs had developed by the middle of the 17th century. This wonderful map is an artist's impression of a bird's eye view of the still-separate burghs of Edinburgh and Canongate. While there's artist's license in the stylised buildings and gardens, the map is accurately scaled, and clearly outlines the fish-shape which gave the Old Town its nickname 'the gutted haddie' (haddock).

The walled city of Edinburgh stretched along the ridge from Castle Rock to the Netherbow Port, the gated building which spanned the Royal Mile at the crossroads made by modern Jeffrey and St Mary's Streets. Today there's still a close and a pub there called 'World's End' - clearly Edinburghers felt that venturing across St Mary's Wynd to Canongate was a journey too far!

World's End was the end of Edinburgh

Five centuries after its foundation, Edinburgh was choc-a-bloc, the medieval backlands almost completely built over, and barely a postage stamp of cultivatable soil was to be seen. By the beginning of the 17th century, Edinburgh was the most congested city in Europe, and yet by the end of the same century, its population had quadrupled. Constrained by its geography and city walls, the only option was to build up. In these early 'skyscrapers' of up to 12 - 14 storeys, rich and poor lived together, quite literally in the same buildings: a wealthy family might take the first and second floors, with servants on the ground floor, and a gradation of society took the upper floors, perhaps a merchant family, then craftsmen and a seamstress, up to the pauper who might live in the garret. This must have given burgh-dwellers a certain psychology: neighbours might not always like or approve of each other, but they had to rub along together, all speaking Scots as they passed on the stairway.

It could be a hazardous existence, and fire and pestilence were common. Certainly Edinburgh's High Street was not an environment for pretty gardens - or even functional yards. However, look closely at the Rothiemay map (see map 2) which shows one large, formal garden just east of the Castle, on the south-facing slope between the Lawnmarket and Cowgate; this may be the garden for Riddles Court, built in 1590 by Baillie John McMorran, the wealthiest merchant in the city. Then there is a 'fringe' of gardens to the south on the Pleasance (the word means 'secluded garden' in Scots and gave its name to the street), around the newly built George Heriot's Hospital (the name for a charitable school), and around the foot of Castle Rock.

The heyday of Canongate gardens
Look east of the Netherbow Port to Canongate, and the Rothiemay map shows a very different picture: a continuous line of buildings clustered along the main street, punctuated

only by short closes providing access to large gardens behind, each with well-mannered planting in the formal parterre style.

While Edinburgh was bursting at the seams, Canongate seems positively decorous. Like its larger neighbour, Canongate's long line of buildings housed a melée of people living close together - merchants and craftsmen, laundrywomen and

17th century Canongate gardens

butchers, shoemakers and embroiderers, herbalists and gardeners. In the 17th century they were joined by the aristocracy. Attracted by the large open backlands and proximity to Holyrood Palace, noble families built townhouses along - or, more usually, just behind - the main street, with large, walled, formal gardens behind. The layout may be reminiscent of the medieval backlands, but the homely vegetable plots and kailyards of preceding centuries were now superseded by large walled gardens with formal parterres and lavish orchards. Properties such as Moray House (c1625), Acheson House (1633) and Queensberry House (c1667) were the Canongate residences of aristocrats with rural lands elsewhere. (All three properties still exist and their much diminished gardens continue in different guises.)

Moray House Garden: 'so much beauty in such a frigid clime'
The 17th century was the heyday of Canongate gardens, and the terraced garden at Moray House (10) was considered the most beautiful. Having completed her stylish townhouse

c1625, Mary, Dowager Countess of Home, continued to develop both her house and garden until her death in 1653 when the house passed to her son-in-law the Earl of Murray and was renamed Moray House. Her garden was so famous it continued to be called Lady Home's Yard for many years after her death. The grounds sloped southwards, ending with a wall and gate on to the 'South Back of Canongate' (now Holyrood Road). Clear views south included a towering Arthur's Seat and Salisbury Crags, which together must have dominated the Canongate. Walls, trees and shrubberies gave much-needed shelter (there was a mini-ice age in the 17th century!).

The garden was laid out in the French style with a succession of terraces, connected by handsome stone steps. (The Rothiemay map (reverse back cover) shows four terraces; however, this may have been artist's license.) On the first terrace stood a large tree which may have been planted by Lady Home's gardeners, although legend has it that it was planted much earlier by Mary Queen of Scots, and thus it enjoyed the name Queen Mary's Thorn Tree.

The second terrace was an orchard. The 1646 gardener's inventory for Moray House included 'some two dozen apple trees, about sixty plum and eighty cherry trees, five apricot trees, a damson, a quince and a fig tree'.[5] No doubt the more tender apricots and figs were espaliered against the south-facing wall, which would drop from the first terrace in full sun. When planting free-standing trees, gardeners would often dig a deep, wide hole, pave a circular area at the bottom of the hole with flat stones, backfill with good soil (sometimes adding a dead dog for extra nutrients!); then, as the tree's roots grew, they were forced out, which in turn caused the canopy to spread horizontally, producing shapely and productive trees, and possibly providing shade for the ladies to have their summer

Drawn by Tho. H Shepherd

Engraved by James B Allen

THE LEVEE ROOM IN REGENT MURRAY'S HOUSE, AS SEEN FROM THE GARDEN.

WITH THE REMARKABLE THORN PLANTED BY QUEEN MARY

refreshments. A further terrace may have been a formal garden with 'rooms' given shelter by high evergreen hedges. They'd grow vegetables, soft fruit and herbs there as well as ornamentals.

It's reported that Oliver Cromwell, staying in Moray House in 1650 after defeating the Scots at the Battle of Dunbar, described the garden as 'of so much elegance, and cultivated with so much care, as to vie with those of warmer countries, and perhaps even of England itself ... Scarcely anyone would believe it possible to give so much beauty to a garden in such a frigid clime.'[6]

Canongate gardeners and their plants

For his informative book *Early Scottish Gardeners and their Plants 1650 - 1750*, Forbes W Robertson studied gardeners' lists, estate records, apothecaries' accounts for medicines and household recipes for herbal cures, to glean information about the men who tended the gardens of the well-to-do throughout Scotland, and the types of plants they grew.[7] We're given a picture of gardens which were both productive and beautiful, with highly skilled, resourceful - though usually badly paid - gardeners, employed as part of the traditional complement of servants, and bound by strict rules as to pay and what they could and could not take from the land. Some were granted an allowance of vegetables, others were given a patch to cultivate for their own use. Skills and knowledge were often passed from father to son.

Gardeners in neighbouring estates were in regular contact and often bought or exchanged plants from one another. For example, the gardener at Ravelston (lying about four miles to the northwest of Canongate and now well within Edinburgh's boundaries) records plant exchanges with the gardener at 'Surgeon's Yard' and Heriot's Hospital (both in the area we now call the Old Town).

The gardens were important to the local economy, too, with several seedsmen and nurserymen running successful businesses. Henry Ferguson, a seedsman based 'a little above the head of Black Friers Wynd' (now Blackfriars Street) was probably the first in Scotland to advertise using a broadsheet in 1681. Ferguson's business thrived, and his 1691 catalogue listed seeds for fifty varieties of vegetables, another fifty of herbs, one hundred ornamentals and fifty trees. Modern organic gardeners trying their hand with green manures (where quick-growing crops are grown from seed, then dug into the soil) might note that Ferguson's catalogue offered five types of 'seeds to improve land': 'Clover Grass, San-Foin, La Lucern, Canarie Seed, and Hemp Seed'. Finally, the catalogue lists a selection of garden tools and teapots, along with 'the Catalogue of Plants in the Physical Garden' and a variety of medications, including 'the Plain and Purging Elixerated Spirits of Scurvy-Gras and Worm Powder for Children'. Ferguson's business sounds like a cross between a modern garden centre and apothecary.

What did they grow?
The best-kept records were for vegetables, with a number of new varieties being introduced from the early 17th century onwards. It's very likely that Canongate gardeners grew onions (probably several varieties), leeks, turnips, carrots, beetroot (red, white and green), cabbages (white, red and Savoy), cauliflower, kale, peas (early, maincrop and sugar), beans, asparagus, celery, spinach, and artichoke. 'Sallet' or 'salleting' were general names for the young leaves of quite a large number of different plants; cucumber and salad onion (called 'syboes', as my own mother did fifty years ago) were also a common seed order. Scorzonera

and skirret were widely grown root vegetables until 'the rise in the popularity of the potato sealed their fate' in the 18th century.

Accounts of culinary herbs were good, too; a long list includes caraway, chervil, dill, marjoram, sage and thyme. Tender herbs such as basil, coriander and cumin were grown on a hot bed, a method of raising early or tender crops in which gardeners of the time excelled. Usually in January, gardeners made their hot beds by digging in a large mass of fresh, strawy manure from the stables to give bottom heat over several weeks as it rotted. The hot beds gave gardeners a headstart: they sowed seeds for early crops of peas, radishes, carrots, spinach, lettuce and tender flowers in February; even cucumbers and melons were planted directly in a hotbed under glass in late winter. This seems alarmingly early for modern gardeners in Scotland!

As we've seen in Moray House (10), Scots gardeners were highly skilled in growing fruit, in a tradition going all the way back to 12th century monastery and abbey orchards, where the monks trained local gardeners in skills which originated in France. With their long cultivation in Scotland, Forbes Robertson found excellent records of the names of apples, pears, plums, cherries, apricots, peaches and nectarines and detailed orchard inventories, often of very old - and sweet - varieties.

Ornamentals

The evidence for ornamental plants is patchy, with seed orders often meriting a general order for '20 sorts of flower seeds'. Annual flowers were the preserve of the women of the house, and sometimes the accounts even refer to 'seeds for my Lady'. Before the introduction of foreign species, the variety of herbaceous plants commonly grown was

Summer house and Salisbury Crags from Moray House Garden

A SUMMER-HOUSE IN REGENT MURRAY'S GARDEN, WHERE THE UNION OF THE
TWO KINGDOMS WAS SIGNED.

quite modest, consisting of mostly native species transferred to the garden from the wild, such as primroses, cowslips and cranesbills. However, many varieties of shrub roses were popular. We can actually see this for ourselves in Dunbar's Close Garden (11), which grows mainly modern varieties of plants actually grown in 17th century Scotland: in the long east-facing border, the old roses including *Rosa centifolia* (the 'rose with a hundred leaves', highly sought-after at the time) and *Rosa moschata* (the musk rose, a fragrant shrub of long provenance and eastern origin) bloom only once, in June, but like many old roses make up for this with a heady scent and lovely autumn hips. *Rosa alba* is believed to have been the White Rose chosen as an emblem by the Jacobites of the next century; some think it may also have been the White Rose of York.

Bulbs and tubers were very popular. In Dunbar's Close, a large number of crown imperials (*Fritallaria imperialis*) make a real talking point in spring, with their strange, large, spiky flowers in both yellow and red; a little later, in May, they are superseded by clumps of the old white iris, *Iris florentina*, grown around 17th century Florence for its orris root which was used as a fixative in perfume; its beautiful, exuberant flower still features in Florence's coat of arms. Although planted in generous numbers today, bulbs were so expensive that even the wealthy of that time would own only one or two of each variety.

The 17th century was of course the beginning of the great plant hunters, when fortunes were made and lost in the search around the world for exotic plants to be sold to eager gardeners back home. The beautiful tulip tree, *Liriodendron tulipifera*, growing in the centre of the parterre at the entrance of Dunbar's Close, for example, is a native of the eastern seaboard of North America. It had been introduced to Britain by John Tradescant around 1650 and may well have been used as a fashionable specimen tree in Scottish gardens.

Grey Friars, wise women and physic gardens

Our ancestors depended on plants for the care and prevention of disease; the majority of the world still does. In Scotland, as in the rest of Europe, there have been three main growers and users of medicinal herbs: medieval monks, traditional healers, and professionals including apothecaries and physicians. The Old Town has borne witness to all of these.

The Grey Friars

Around 1447, six brothers of the Order of Saint Francis of Assisi were invited to Edinburgh from the Netherlands, initially to found a centre of learning on sloping ground on the south-eastern end of the Grassmarket. They were embarrassed by the grandeur of the

friary, which had been built for them on the orders of James I; after all, they were Observantines ('strictly observant') and had taken a vow of poverty.

Called Grey Friars after the colour of their habits, they established a medicinal herb garden to care for the poor and sick of the Grassmarket. They joined the Dominican Black Friars whose monastic garden lay just to the west, and the Augustinians at Holyrood Abbey.

Monasteries had provided health care for

Herbs grow again at Greyfriars

centuries, first through the Celtic Church, then through powerful orders such as the Augustinians, who had been invited to Scotland from France by David I to set up monasteries and abbeys, mainly along the Border country. By the 12th century, Scotland boasted a network of at least 150 hospitals attached to religious houses, many of them connected to a wider European network of monastic health care based on plants. The largest and probably the most famous hospital was at Soutra, about fifteen miles south of the Old Town. Recent archaeological excavation has identified 300 non-native plant species on Soutra Hill, most of them introduced by the monks. Soutra's decline followed a major scandal in the 1460s, when a renegade Master was deposed after offences were reported to Papal authorities. The Scottish Crown re-assigned the hospital estates to the new Trinity College Hospital in Edinburgh, a monastic hospital and garden on the site of Waverley Station (two centuries later, this site became a physic garden).

The Grey Friars would have been linked into this 'state of the art' knowledge. Unlike Soutra, no records remain of the Grey Friars' plants or treatments, probably because in 1559 their friary was destroyed by Reformers and the friars were forced to flee. Three years later, the Town Council was granted permission by Mary Queen of Scots to use the Grey Friars' herb garden as a burial ground (4).

Persecution

In 1597, Janet Stewart of Canongate was charged and convicted of witchery, sorcery and incantations. The complaint against her was made by Andro Pennycuick who stated in court that he had gone to visit her for advice as to his sickness, and that she had 'dune him nae guid'. Janet was found guilty of curing (!) others with poultices of herbs and draughts of white wine, and was executed by strangling then burnt at the stake at Edinburgh Castle.

The 16th and 17th centuries were tragic times of religious persecution, witch hunting, and a mania to stamp out so-called 'devilish practices' throughout Europe. Folk healers were particularly vulnerable: if a cure (or non-cure) seemed inexplicable, then it must have been the devil's work. Three hundred women and men were burned at the stake at Edinburgh Castle, with at least 1,000 in Scotland as a whole (some estimates are as high as 4,500); 80% of these were women, and many were folk healers, convicted of such things as giving herbs to relieve the pain of childbirth.

There is a dearth of information about which herbs were regularly grown for medicinal use at this time, in spite of the widespread use of healing plants by all classes of society. (The situation was to improve with the cataloguing of Edinburgh's principal physic garden in the next century.) It's likely that traditional knowledge of plant remedies, still strong in many rural areas, waned as people moved into towns. Even when they had the knowledge, it would be difficult to find the right plants. Where then did ordinary people go for health advice and treatment in 16th and 17th century Edinburgh and Canongate? Most could not afford physicians' fees. Some would consult the dozens of apothecaries who mixed and sold plant remedies, and barber surgeons - whose trade was linked with barbers as both worked with sharp knives! - who served part of their apprenticeship in apothecaries' shops.

But were there also wise women able to treat their neighbours in the closes? And if so, how effective were they? Perhaps no-one now can give a definitive answer: the poor, after all, did not write history. There may be, however, an answer of sorts - or at least a hypothesis - in the plants themselves. Janet Stewart was living in Canongate and administering herbal treatments at exactly the historical moment when gardeners of wealthy aristocrats were starting to lay out formal gardens, probably within sight of Janet's home, using plants which we can see today in Dunbar's Close Garden (11).

A couple of years ago I strolled there with Julia Cook, a qualified medical herbalist, who, looking closely at the plants, remarked that the vast majority have medicinal uses which were well-known to herbalists at the time. They included varieties of honeysuckle, marigolds, hollyhocks, roses, lavender, Solomon's Seal and rue. Many herbs we'd use in cooking were grown for medicinal uses too. For example, the lovage (*Levisticum officinale*) growing lustily in one of the yew compartments is closely related to the shorter Scots lovage (*Ligusticum scoticum*) which was found all along the coast of Scotland, and brought into gardens as a culinary herb; in her book *The Scots Herbal: the Plant Lore of Scotland*, Tess Darwin records that Scots lovage 'was recommended as a tonic, appetiser and against scurvy and consumption, often cooked with lamb broth and alexanders, although the strong, not particularly pleasant taste did not make it popular'.[8] Its name 'lovage' derives from its use as an aphrodisiac.

Wise woman and foxglove detail, Witches' Fountain

With or without permission, who might have been using these plants in the Canongate? Local apothecaries, almost certainly, the lady of the house, probably; and perhaps also Janet Stewart and others like her who had little means other than the knowledge they'd brought from their rural roots? Of course, this is speculation; what cannot be doubted is the effect of witch hunts and urbanisation on the practice of herbal medicine; as Darwin concludes: 'Herbal medicine survived, but never regained the status it had and still has in many parts of the world.'

Physic gardens

Physicians, surgeons, barber surgeons and apothecaries all practised in 17th century Edinburgh and Canongate. Although administering to different clienteles, these groups had much in common: each depended on a knowledge of plants, and jealously guarded their status. Each group had genuine practitioners, but also quacks and charlatans, making money from increasingly bizarre 'remedies'. Towards the end of the 17th century, the best-intentioned practitioners in each group recognised a need for good, healthy, locally grown plant material, and for gardens as a resource for teaching their apprentices and students.

The first physic garden in Scotland was established in 1656 by the Incorporation of Surgeons and Barber Surgeons in the grounds of their hall at Curryhill in Edinburgh's Old Town (the garden was on the south side of today's Infirmary Street). Then, in 1661, Heriot's Hospital (a charitable school for 'puir faitherless bairns') put part of their grounds aside for medicinal herbs; this was referred to as an apothecary garden, and for a while allowed access to anyone who wished to study the plants. Most significantly, in 1670 two Edinburgh physicians and botanists, Robert Sibbald and Andrew Balfour, took a lease on a piece of ground adjacent to Holyrood Abbey (16). With the brilliant and virtually self-taught James Sutherland as head gardener, St Anne's Yard soon had 900 plants. As Sibbald and Balfour had hoped, they were soon producing enough plants for their own herbal preparations and for sale to fellow physicians and apothecaries. Initially, the surgeon-apothecaries resented the new garden, but before long they were sending their apprentices to be taught by Sutherland.[9]

The space soon became too small and in 1676 another plot of land was leased at Trinity College Hospital, on the site of Waverley Station, where over 2,000 plants were grown. Although undoubtedly beautiful when in season, the garden was arranged systematically for instruction and identification rather than as a pleasure garden. Three plots grew plants ordered according to their botanical classification; in a fourth plot, plants were arranged in alphabetical order as an aide memoir to medical students. A fifth plot had a pond for aquatic plants, and a sixth was an arboretum with shrubs and trees. Dr Sibbald wrote that almost all plants known at the time for the cure of sickness and disease were grown, including plants from both hemispheres; rarer and more exotic plants were protected under glass.

During the late 17th and early 18th centuries, there were at least seven physic gardens in the Old Town.[10] Early 18th century maps show a physic garden immediately south of Fountain Court (7), in exactly the current site of Saint Patrick's Church (physicians are known to have met for a time in Fountain Court); the garden was so popular with the general public that the physicians had it fenced off, entry only being possible with a key obtainable from the College.

Botany, medicine and the Scottish Enlightenment

In 1763, the plants from Trinity College were carefully transferred to a new five-acre site at the top of Leith Walk, away from the Old Town's pollution, and the foundations of the Royal Botanic Garden Edinburgh were laid. The physic gardens are a reminder that botany and medicine were once completely intertwined, and that a knowledge of plants and their uses was an essential part of medical education. Plantsmen and botanists were important players in the Scottish Enlightenment of the 18th century; Jane Corrie explains: 'The

Enlightenment thinkers wanted to systematise knowledge. Having a physic garden was seen as a symbol of progressive thought, and had extraordinary professional cachet for physicians and botanists.' The quality of Edinburgh's physic gardens is often cited as one of the reasons that the city became a centre of excellence for teaching medicine.

Changing fortunes: 18th, 19th and 20th centuries

In the 18th century, life continued to be claustrophobic, unsafe and downright unhealthy for all classes in Edinburgh. Even the Canongate was slowly following suit; while wealthy people continued to build large townhouses with generous gardens - Milton House (now the site of Royal Mile Primary School) and Whitefoord House were among those developed in 18th century Canongate - several of the established grand houses such as Queensberry House were divided into flats for professional families (especially lawyers whose livelihood was based in the Courts in Edinburgh), and previously elegant garden space was gradually taken up by new tenements and the small industries which began to thrive in Canongate.

Seedsmen and nurserymen continued to play an important role in the Canongate economy. In 1689, William Millar, a devout Quaker, took up the post of Head Gardener at the Abbey of Holyroodhouse (16). He soon began to use some of his allotted ground to raise plants for sale, later going into partnership with his second son William. Nurserymen were enjoying a lucrative and expanding market, as new, fashionable plants were introduced from overseas and large country estates were created. Father and son built up a thriving élite business which supplied seeds, trees and shrubs to estates all over Scotland. For the best part of a century, the 'William Millars at the Abbey' played an influential role in the Scottish nursery business. By the time the third William Millar inherited, the family had amassed a great fortune.[11]

Just half a mile up Canongate High Street, however, Edinburgh was stewing. Not surprisingly, many of those with the wherewithal were looking for a way out. Moving to George Square, completed in 1763 just a mile or so to the south, became a fashionable escape. The Norloch (on the site of Princes Street Gardens) was drained in 1759 and North Bridge was completed in 1772, opening up the development of the New Town. Slowly but surely, the nobility and professional classes deserted the old closes and wynds in favour of New Town grandeur and improved facilities. It wasn't at first a stampede, more a slow drift over about eighty years; indeed some of the gentry wanted to stay in what became the Old Town - where there was life in the streets and taverns, and shops where a customer could buy almost anything - in preference to the more decorous New Town.

However, by the mid 19th century, the exodus of the upper and middle classes was complete, their places taken by much poorer people - many from Ireland and the Scottish Highlands - coming into the city in large numbers for employment in the new railway, breweries, printing and publishing and other growing industries, and attracted by the Old Town's cheap rents. Edinburgh's natural features gave its social inequalities a geographical twist: the poor on the Old Town ridge and the wealthier in the New Town looked suspiciously at each other over the newly landscaped, private West Princes Street Garden. By 1861, the Royal Mile had its highest population ever, of at least 40,000. Amid growing concern over public health risks, the City fathers actually sought new legislation (the 1867 Improvement Act) which gave them powers to improve the insanitary and squalid conditions.

The Chambers Scheme of the same year had mixed success: the elegant Chambers Street was built on the south side of the Old Town, yet a policy of slum clearance resulted in the demolition of nearly one-third of the Old Town housing stock, and the loss of many fine historic buildings. Slum landlords received generous compensation, yet there was no obligation to re-house tenants or to build on cleared sites, so displaced tenants had little choice but to move on to nearby properties which in turn became subdivided. The answer to this was council housing: High School Yards near the Cowgate, ready for its first tenants in 1897, was the first municipal housing in Edinburgh, followed by Tron Square (5) in 1900.[12]

Chessels Court: an example of Old Town fortunes

The social history of one rather beautiful court just off the Canongate captures the changing fortunes of the Old Town from the 18th century until the present day. Chessels Court (9) was built by Archibald Chesils in the 1740s. Chesils was a wright (a Scots word for

Chessels Building today

master carpenter) and a property developer. He may also, in modern parlance, have been a bit of a wideboy: there were fairly regular complaints about his workmanship and disputes about his rights to land![13] However, he was a man with a vision: in this newly acquired land set back from the main street he planned to sell property to and for both rich and poor. He designed and built the graceful, flatted Chessels Building on the south of the court as 'gentlemen's mansionhouse apartments', some with extensive private gardens to the rear. On the east side, where a 1960s block of flats is today, Chesils built a block of single-room family flats called ` single ends' in Scotland. These buildings, with their diverse residents, faced the square, which Chesils planned as a gracious, light-filled courtyard, allowing the wealthier residents all the benefits of living in the city, while being detached from the unpleasant noise and stench of the street.

However, in spite of some prestigious early residents (James Boswell the writer being one), Chesils' project failed. As wealthier residents left for the New Town, poorer families moved into Chessels Building, and the spacious apartments became divided and subdivided, until many of the mansion apartments themselves became a warren of single ends. By the 19th century, tenements were built in the courtyard and all round the square, replacing Chesils' airy space with dark closes. Chessels Court, like much of the Old Town, became an overcrowded slum, surrounded by small industry: the Ordinance Survey map of 1877 shows a timberyard to the west of Chessels Court, with St Mary's Brewery and a tannery to the south, making this once-graceful court a particularly foul-smelling place to live.

The Court fared no better for much of the 20th century: a retired postman told me that in the 1960s, there were so many doors to deliver to that Chessels Court was one postman's shift! By then, the fabric of Chessels Building was literally falling down, and Edinburgh Corporation had to act: given the stark choice to demolish or restore, they chose to restore to a very high standard, initially to provide high quality council flats. The architect, Robert Hurd, wanted to respect the old buildings, not as museum exhibits, but as a way of keeping the Court alive for the 20th century and beyond. Internally, Chesils' original plasterwork, timberwork, and - in some of the larger flats - original panel paintings by the painter and decorator James Norrie, were beautifully restored. Externally, Hurd demolished Victorian tenements, built an arched arcade on to the main street, allowing light in once again, and reintroduced the colour-washed walls of the medieval town.

Visit Chessels Court today, and what you see is pretty much the restoration of the 1960s. Council flats have gone into private ownership, yet the Court retains a mixture of tenants and home-owners and a sense of community, and surprises visitors with its greenery hidden behind Canongate tenements. The development showed that new life - and green space - could be re-introduced into a derelict area of the Old Town.

'Children's gardens in the dark places of the Old Town'

Over the 19th and early 20th centuries, there was precious little green space in the Old Town. Great reforming improvements such as the Victorian parks and working class action in the allotment movement largely passed the Old Town by. However, in the early years of the 20th century two pioneering initiatives brought gardens into the Old Town.[14]

The Free Kindergartens

In the summer of 1906, a determined young woman called Lileen Hardy approached Canon Laurie of Old St Paul's Church in Jeffrey Street to discuss the idea of a 'child garden'. Both wanted to provide an environment where pre-school children could thrive, away from the street or dark homes where many spent their days while their parents worked and their older siblings went to school. Three years earlier, in November 1903, the first nursery school in Scotland, the Edinburgh Free Kindergarten, had opened in Galloway's Entry in Canongate; in 1906 it moved over the road to Reid's Court, then a crumbling mansion with private gardens to the rear (now restored as Canongate Kirk's handsome manse).

A lesson in horticulture, Saint Saviour's Child Garden

Soon after, in November 1906, Miss Hardy opened Saint Saviour's Child Garden Nursery in an old mission hall in nearby Brown's Close, with three children. A garden where the children would tend plants with specially made child-size tools, look after class pets, and follow much of their daily routine outdoors, was (and still is) a central part of the Free Kindergartens' philosophy: quite an ambition in the Canongate of the time, yet, as she describes in her book *The Diary of a Free Kindergarten*, Miss Hardy lost no time in the task.

'Our garden is a piece of waste ground lying just outside our back door. There were until recently old houses standing on it. When we took it over, it was littered with debris of all kinds, broken bottles, old tin cans, old boots, hats, stays, bones, potato peelings, two dead puppies, and one dead cat. ... It took three scavengers' carts to get it removed.'[15]

With help from fathers and older brothers in pickaxing and digging, and red ash surfaces laid by the City Gardener, Miss Hardy riddled earth and begged plants from supporters, until, by summer, she reports:

'Our garden is just lovely. It is about 90 by 20 feet, two red ash playgrounds, one getting morning sun, the other afternoon, one piece of lawn (real grass), lots of flower-borders, and a jolly big sand-bed. Some of the older ones are beginning to observe opening buds without direction, and one keen young naturalist gave a leap into the air when he discovered his seeds coming up.'

The neighbours stopped throwing their ash and rubbish on the developing garden, and made sure no-one else did. Miss Hardy was soon able to open in the afternoons as well as mornings to care for her growing class of children.

Move to Chessels Court In 1908, Saint Saviour's moved to the faded grandeur of the ground floor flat in Chessels Buildings (9). Miss Hardy was delighted: 'The house is all the kindergarten's own and admirably suited for our purposes.' Just as importantly, the flat came with its own private garden 'on the south side, sheltered, and, for the district, marvellously secluded. In front of us there is nothing but breweries on a much lower level, so that it is practically open, and we have a fine view of Salisbury Crags.' By the next spring, the new garden was thriving, with flower beds and vegetables, a rope ladder and swings. Soon, the Child Garden's roll was up to fifty, and a garden shelter had become a preparatory school for eight of the older children who were almost ready to go up to primary school. Another, larger, shelter bought with donations allowed the youngest children to have an afternoon sleep outdoors all summer, whatever the weather, and became classroom and lunchroom too.

Lileen Hardy's *The Diary of a Free Kindergarten* gives an insight into children's lives in the Old Town of more than a century ago, a time when lack of boots to wear - often because boots were in the pawn - was the most common reason for a child to miss school. Life in the shadow of looming tenements could also result in a kind of nature poverty. While preparing the first garden, Miss Hardy realises that 'the children did not know what grass is. When I told them we were going to have grass in the garden, they thought I was talking about glass. Now with the turf before them they have no name for it. And the King's Park [Arthur's Seat] is only ten minute's distance from some of their homes, much less for some.' One February, she writes: 'We climbed the Radical Road this evening to do homage to the sun. It was the first time the children had seen the daily miracle of the sunset.'

Over the next thirty years, other pioneer child garden nurseries opened in Edinburgh, seven

Little gardeners, Saint Saviours Child Garden Nursery

in the Old Town, including the Grassmarket Child Garden (opened in 1925 by a family trust) and Cowgate Nursery School (opened in 1937 by the Church of Scotland Mission); several of these early child gardens continue as nurseries under the auspices of the city's Education Department. That unusual little phrase 'child garden' is still used in the Old Town.

Saint Saviours Child Garden Nursery continued under the management of Old Saint Paul's Church until 1977. Today the flat and garden are owned privately; a pear tree mentioned in Miss Hardy's *Diary* still grows there, an old, gnarled witness to all the changes of the last century and more, and still producing literally hundreds of pears each year.

The Geddes Gardens
On Friday 9th May 1909, a children's garden was opened off South Castle Wynd (now renamed Patrick Geddes Steps), just behind the White Hart pub on the Grassmarket. There was a fanciful ceremony which started with a procession from Castlehill led by the 'Pied Piper' and continued with local boys planting a tree. Scores of ladies and gentlemen supporters in smart clothes watched girls in white dresses dancing round a maypole, neighbours cheered from tenement windows, and boys perched precariously on a high dividing wall for the best view.

The next day, The Edinburgh Evening News reported the story, complete with photograph, under the headline 'The Waste Spaces of the Old Town: A Laudable Scheme Inaugurated'. The land, lately a rubbish heap, belonged to the Public House Trust Company, and had been let to the organisers at the nominal rent of one shilling per annum.

The White Hart Garden was the first of around ten children's gardens created in waste spaces and gap sites by the rather unpromisingly named Outlook Tower Open Spaces

Committee in the years just before the First World War. Their work was inspired by a prominent intellectual and a 'weel kent face' in Edinburgh at the time: Patrick Geddes.

Patrick Geddes and the Outlook Tower

Patrick Geddes (1856-1932) was a biologist, sociologist, environmentalist, social reformer and townplanner who advocated that cities could be healthy and inspiring places to live. He and his wife Anna lived in the Old Town for forty years, first in slum housing in James Court, later in the arts and crafts-inspired Ramsay Garden (1), which Geddes himself had commissioned in 1892-3, partly to encourage a social mix in the area by attracting professional people.

For thirty years, slum improvement in Edinburgh had meant wholesale demolition followed by building boom, moving the poorest tenants on to other slum properties, and even making them homeless. Geddes took a much gentler approach which he termed 'conservative surgery', working with architects to retain and restore historic buildings, making smaller changes to improve conditions such as opening up courtyards to let light in, or adding balconies to give some outdoor space. James Court and Wardrop Court off the Lawnmarket are lasting examples of his approach.[16]

Geddes was a great educator and persuader. Inspired by a visit to the Camera Obscura on Castlehill, he bought the building in 1892 and renamed it the Outlook Tower (1), part museum, part university, part call to action. Geddes, who coined the now-famous phrase 'Think global, act local', wanted visitors to the Outlook Tower to see Edinburgh clearly within the world, and then act to improve it. Often he would show visitors round himself, making them climb at speed to the top of the spiral staircase, keeping them for a while in a darkened room, red-faced and out of breath, before suddenly exposing them to the light of the roof terrace to look over Edinburgh, the Pentland Hills, the Firth of Forth and beyond. He'd then usher them down into the camera obscura itself, where they'd see the city literally through a different lens. The mechanics are a cross between a giant pinhole camera and a periscope. At the top of the tower is a dark chamber with a mirror on top which reflects light downwards, passing through three lenses before projecting an image of the city on to a large white table. The guide turns and tilts the mirror to give a 360° tour of Edinburgh.[17] At a time just before cinema, this real-time moving image of the city streets below must have seemed magical; just as today, guests would be invited to 'pick up' a passer-by in the palm of their hand.

Finally, the awed visitor would descend the spiral staircase to see and discuss other displays showing Scotland, Europe and the world. The Outlook Tower pioneered the educational use of photographs and lantern slides, and a favourite topic was the 'before' and 'after' images of the children's gardens being created nearby.

Gardens vs 'nature starvation'

Geddes, a biologist by training, had been brought up in rural Perthshire and that early closeness to nature influenced him all his life. Gardens and gardening to combat what he termed 'nature starvation' in the slums were part of his vision for the Old Town. However, it was relatively late in his career, when well into his fifties, that his colleagues and family began to create Old Town gardens.

Over 1909-10, the Outlook Tower Open Spaces Committee surveyed the whole of the Old Town, mapping 75 potential garden sites totalling ten acres, mainly in wasteland and gap sites left by demolition and rebuilding. Norah Geddes, Anna and Patrick's twenty-one-year-old daughter, designed and planted many of the gardens; Strathclyde University Library holds a large folder of her original garden sketches with the inscription in her writing 'Edinburgh Open Spaces, carried out at one time or another'. Norah later married Frank Mears, a young architect who carried out the Open Spaces survey. Over the next two or three years, about ten of the 75 spaces were made into gardens for children, managed and paid for by the Committee, but sometimes gardened by local schools or children's clubs.

The local primary school on Castlehill took on the White Hart Garden and the nearby King's Wall Garden (also off South Castle Wynd, and so called because the space is bordered on the north side by one of the ancient city walls). According to a news report of 11 July 1911, the school took their gardening very seriously:

'On the slope that rises so abruptly from Grassmarket to the Castle is situated an experimental garden, which is worked by the scholars of Castlehill Public School, under the direction of Mr Craigie, the headmaster, and Mr Kippen, one of the assistant masters. Vegetable plots are arranged on a broad border about 100 feet in length and by 7 feet wide. The crops consist of potatoes, peas, beans, cauliflower, savoys, turnips, leeks, onions, carrots, lettuces, radishes, etc. ... Some of the crops are most promising, and give evidence of good culture and great care. ... In country districts, it is usual for each set of boys to get a plot, but this is impossible in the very centre of a city, and the boys in relays take the work.'[18] The girls used the produce in cookery lessons.

On 1 April 1912 Miss Hardy writes about the Geddes garden created in Chessels Court: 'A wonderful transformation has been made. ... The Outlook Tower has cleared away the

Norah Geddes's sketch plan for King's Wall Garden

89

refuse, removed remains of fallen houses, and laid out a delightful garden. The dignity which the large open space gives to the really fine old houses is very striking. ... We have the pleasure of it as we pass to and from the Canongate; and the sense of joy and relief which the sight of it gives can hardly be realised except by those who habitually suffer from the depressing effect of ugly surroundings.'[19]

Through hard times

In the early years, some fifty lady volunteers organised play sessions. This number dwindled in later years, and Open Spaces leaflets record a constant plea for donations of money and plants, and in particular for volunteers. During the First World War, dark streets and tragic losses took their toll. Yet, in 1918, the Committee reports: 'Notwithstanding the lack of helpers, several of the gardens have been open to the children. King's Wall, in particular, has been a great delight and interest to many children ... many of the children attend regularly, and are greatly disappointed when no-one appears to open the gardens for them.'

Perhaps the most successful garden was West Port (3), a steeply terraced space opened jointly with Candlemaker Row Garden on 4 June 1910 by Provost L. P. Brown amid applause from a large crowd in the newly made terraces, on the street, and at the windows of the neighbouring tenements. A little girl handed the Lord Provost a posie of the garden's first flowers, and a sepia photograph captures her with Patrick Geddes and a group of dignitaries. West Port thrived because it attracted local support, and because it provided outdoor recreation for all ages. A Hut Club House was built which served boys' and girls' sports clubs and a company of Boy Scouts; a 1926 Open Spaces leaflet entitled 'Gardens in the Dark Places of the Old Town' described the Hut as the 'meeting place of a Sports Club formed by Mr A Thomson of 17 West Port for lads between the ages of 14 and 20, who as children frequented the Garden. At Christmas, the Hut arranged a tree and entertainment for 250 children of the district which gave great pleasure.' The garden continued until after World War Two. Some local residents still refer to this spot as 'the Geddes garden'.

20th century - present

The City Architect's Report of 1945 noted that only 7% of the homes on the Royal Mile were 'up to modern standards'. This is of course within living memory: many people have told me of their 1940s, 50s or 60s childhood in a wee flat (always called a 'house' in Edinburgh) with no bathroom, and a shared toilet on the stair. They played mainly in the street or gap sites (the backgreen often out of bounds because of stern neighbours - perhaps a peculiarly Edinburgh tradition!) although several people remember sneaking off to the glorious green slopes of Arthur's Seat, always in fear that someone might tell their mother they'd strayed too far! Several enlightened renewal schemes such as Chessels Court (9) provided good social housing - and green space - in the Old Town, but from the middle of the 20th century, in yet another exodus, families moved out to new council housing around the city - often with the enticing prospect of a garden.

Fountain Court Garden was developed in the 1980s

The Old Town was beginning to change in other ways. The Edinburgh Fringe started in 1947 when eight theatre groups turned up uninvited to perform at the newly formed Edinburgh International Festival. When the Edinburgh Fringe Society was formed in 1959, the obvious place to open their box office was the Royal Mile. Now claimed to be the largest arts festival on earth, running 2,453 different shows in August 2010, the Royal Mile remains at the heart of the Fringe.

The Old Town now is largely seen as a mixed, lively place to live - perhaps too lively for some! This section has emphasised the shifts in living conditions because these changing fortunes have made the Old Town what it is today - and makes the fact that there are gardens a cause of surprise to many people! The gardens we see today started with the development of Dunbar's Close (11) by the Mushroom Trust, completed and handed over to Edinburgh Council in 1977, Johnston Terrace Wildlife Garden (2) by Scottish Wildlife Trust in 1982, and the garden for Fountain Court (7) residents by Castlerock Housing Association in the mid-1980s.

With its mixed population and varied gardens, has the Royal Mile perhaps gone full circle from its medieval backlands? It's time to take a look at the present and future of Old Town gardens.

Part Three
Green Shoots

Old Town gardeners are at the heart of this book. Here you'll meet some of the people who've created and maintained gardens, some collectively, some in private space. You'll read about children who are learning to love the natural world right in the city centre, and hear one woman's vision of Old Town gardens in the future: green shoots that will give new life to this amazing place.

A few Old Town gardeners

People in the Old Town garden for many reasons: for the beauty of plants set off by stone walls and cobbles; because the creative outdoor exercise makes them feel better; because gardening gets them out, meeting neighbours and passers-by; or because, among the tenements, they miss the greenery of a childhood garden. Others get a kick from producing food that tastes great, or because trees and shrubs bring bird song into the closes. One gardener tells me that for years, looking after plants has helped her through bouts of depression.

As gardeners they are lucky in some ways: high buildings make these gardens surprisingly sheltered, the stone walls acting like storage heaters and muffling sound; quiet, secluded gardens come alive with bird song, and herbs smell fantastic in such mild and protected places.

Royal Mile gardeners, Coinyie House Close Garden

Liz Edwards is a sprightly woman in her seventies who lives with her husband Tom in Fountain Court's sheltered housing complex (8). Liz is one of the residents who cares for the small, south-facing terraced garden in the Court, making it a favourite place for residents to sit out. She says: 'We've been in Fountain Court for fifteen years and I've gardened there for about seven or eight years. I felt there was no colour and I think people like to look out at a bit of colour. I also love the birds - I've seen more birds this year; they nest in some of our shrubs and in St Patrick's garden next door. It's a rair wee spot for them. Maybe it's my farming background. My dad and granddad were farmers, and I think that's why I love to see things growing. My granddad used to let me potter about and pick his strawberries and tomatoes. Unfortunately veg wouldn't last here - the passers-by would pull them up. A lot of mischief goes on at night around the garden, but as long as they leave the plants alone, they can do what they like!'

Yvonne Farquhar and Faye Sweeney live in and around Coinyie House Close (7). They've been friends for nearly thirty years, as Yvonne remembers: 'I was the first to move into this block of flats 29 years ago. Faye, who lives across the court, started gardening with one pot she placed at the side of the courtyard. I got talking with her, and I added another two. After twenty years, we had well over two hundred pots. It took us two hours to water them!' Since the courtyard was revamped as a community garden in 2009-10, Yvonne and Faye have spent many hours replanting and giving away the plants they've tended for decades.

Their neighbour Anne Jones was one of half a dozen people who attended gardening classes in 2010, and now has one of the individual plots around the courtyard. Anne says: 'My main object was to make a little private space like a cottage garden. This is of course not recommended by the garden books for an urban garden! I was given many plants from Faye and Yvonne such as honeysuckle and conifers. I have always liked the idea of growing food. Last year I planted rhubarb and strawberry plants, plus raspberry and blackcurrant bushes. I was given onions and potatoes by one of the others on the gardening class. After seeing beetroot growing in Yvonne's plot and loving the colours, I have them this year.'

Since moving to Chessels Court (9) thirty years ago, Anja Amsel has been active in several Old Town community organisations. Anja believes the little Jardins Publics garden where residents grow herbs at the corner of the Court has improved community spirit:

'In 2007 Jardins Publics set up an initiative to beautify an area that had been neglected. It's now an attractive garden space and lovely seating spot; as well as local residents, people who work locally sit and have lunch, and tourists enjoy a rest there.' It's also given people confidence to garden: 'There has been a definite legacy for Chessels Court residents too. It has encouraged us to plant up other parts of the Court - we've realised we can colonise these spaces with plants! Every so often we have volunteer parties, for example last Sunday a group of us tidied up the rose bed together. Neighbours have become friends.'

David Lownie became gardener at Dunbar's Close Garden (11) after a long gardening career, first training at Dobbies' Melville Nursery when he left school at fifteen: 'I was there for three years, and got a really good grounding, especially in roses. We took qualifications at night school. I joined Edinburgh Council Parks Department when I was eighteen and stayed there for over thirty years. For a long time, I was Head Gardener at Saughton Park [in west Edinburgh], specialising in roses. We were always in the top two or three in the national trials for rose gardens.'

After retiring from the Parks Department, David was approached about taking on Dunbar's Close, where he has been gardener for ten years: 'It's a very different type of garden. For parks, it was all about colour, lots of bedding plants, with everything uniform. Here it's more subtle - I don't think they had much colour in the 17th century! But I love caring for the yew and box hedging, and the clipped bay trees.' Although David is employed by the Mushroom Trust, Edinburgh Council also provides some support. David certainly has no regrets: 'Fifty years a gardener this year - here's to the next fifty!'

Sylvia von Hartmann is an artist whose inspiration comes from nature. Outside her cottage in White Horse Close, she uses every inch of wall, windowsill and available cobbles to grow mainly container plants. She is also an expert forager: 'I see edible fungi everywhere, even here in the Old Town. I learned by cutting and smelling and eating them. I fry them in butter and parsley, or I string and hang them up to dry then add to soups and stews.' In early autumn, Sylvia can be seen walking down the Royal Mile with armfuls of elder laden with berries: 'Like all my German friends, I have my own secret patch to gather them. We use them to make a soup called *Fliedersuppe* which really sets us up for the winter.'

Elder berries make great soup for an Old Town forager

Not always rosy

Of course, there are lots of spaces calling out for some greenery in the Old Town, and at least one guerrilla gardener has secretly created a colourful - and stylish - little patch just off the Canongate. His name is Matthew and he explains why he's taken this on: 'It brightens up neglected spaces. I think everyone benefits when an otherwise empty piece of ground looks cared-for. Some of my neighbours said it wouldn't last but I got lots of good comments from passers-by and three years later it's still looking great.'

But, before this all sounds too idyllic, let's get back to a more diverse reality: this is Edinburgh's Old Town, the heart of the Edinburgh Fringe, a busy place of street theatre, stag and hen parties, overflowing pubs and restaurants, a subject for photographers on every corner, and tourists from all over the world jostling with the 5,000 or so people who actually live here.

It isn't always rosy on the community front. Neighbours sometimes disagree about the gardens, mainly I think about matters of taste: pots or beds, colourful summer annuals or year-round form and structure, even occasionally whether to have plants in the closes at all. A few years ago, there was a debate amongst conservationists as to how appropriate it might be to have a line of trees along the High Street: for many, this seemed to go against the spirit of the place.

Yet, for many residents, trees are very precious. Until a few years ago, there were a dozen old poplar trees in the Grassmarket; they were pulled down in 2008 when the area was revamped. Grassmarket resident Janet Dick says 'What I notice most is the impact that the loss of the poplars has had on the bird population: there used to be chaffinches in summer and robins in winter. Now it's just seagulls.' Janet points to three mature, very beautiful London plane trees. 'There are bats living in those trees. We hope to encourage them to stay by having bat boxes installed. Bats are protected, and we hope this might help protect the trees.'

'A small place of nature becomes like the world'

On an ancient terraced spot between Grassmarket and Castle Rock, the Scottish Wildlife Trust manages a site to encourage the wildlife that so many city dwellers love to see. Johnston Terrace Wildlife Garden (2) is regularly visited by children from several local nurseries, and I met with three staff members from Cowgate Under Fives Centre to find out why.

Jane Garven originally had the idea of these regular visits in 2009: 'The nursery opens for 52 weeks in the year, and even though we have a lovely garden at the Centre, for a child here all day, it is very special to walk to a wild place. It's the closest wild green space that's accessible on foot. Even the walk there is part of the whole experience - lots of passers-by and shopkeepers talk to the children, and look out for them walking up the High Street and Lawnmarket.' Teresa Bolger mentions another benefit: 'Children now are so often removed from simply exploring open spaces for themselves. When you ask an older person to remember a favourite place where they played, they will nearly always name an outdoor space. That has changed now for many children.'

Finding their own favourite places
The Centre has a rolling programme throughout the year, taking a group of eight

children for a block of six to eight weeks. There is a high adult to child ratio, with two staff and one or two parent volunteers.

Teresa: 'Staff go in advance of every visit to clear away any broken glass, needles and condoms. We leave some of the other, less harmful litter, so that when the group arrives, the first activity is for the children to pick it up using long litter-pickers. We feel this is important, because here the children are learning to take care of their world. The children love that element of freedom; as they move around

Litter picking in Johnston Terrace Wildlife Garden

independently, picking litter, they 'map' the place, investigate the spots that interest them and which they will revisit.' Litter picking done, it's time for play: 'The best way for children to learn is through play. They call the garden "Forest School" or "The Secret Garden". We try to leave them alone and autonomous for a while within this natural space.'

As Donna Begg describes, there's no end to the possibilities for play: 'We are simply providing the opportunity of being there, to let the children explore and find their own favourite spaces. We can't predict what will spark interest on any particular visit. It's never the same. There are rabbits, insects, birds, tadpoles and frogs that might be around. The pond is full of life and changes every time we visit. The log pile is a favourite place for climbing, and there are fungi there called turkey tails. We bring simple resources like clay and paper. We've made kites, and rubbings of the wire mesh over the wooden boardwalk. The children love finding sticks, making up their own uses for them - for dancing, measuring, as a stethoscope or musical instrument. We follow the child's lead. We might then pick up on something one of the children starts doing, for example one boy made a musical instrument out of a stick, and lots of children joined him until they had a little band!'

Nature art using berries

And then there's the weather! Jane says: 'We go in all weathers throughout the year. The only times we've called off is during the Edinburgh Festival, when we almost literally cannot squeeze the children through the crowds on the Royal Mile, and once or twice last winter when the steps were covered in snow and ice. A parent told us that for her child, the best visit was actually a very wet day when we built a shelter from tarpaulin and rope.'

On the last session of every six to eight week block, they light a fire in the brick barbecue and prepare food. There are good things to eat, and in June even a little taste of elderflower. Then afterwards, there's the charcoal for drawing.

Risk and safety

Teresa explains their policy on safety, which involves the children learning to assess risk for themselves: 'We've cleared the site of potentially dangerous items, yet we can't take away all potential dangers. Children do climb to the top of the wych elm, and walk along the uneven wall and wooden boardwalk. Unlike playgrounds where climbing frames might be designed to fit a child's arm span exactly, these need more thought to work out where to put a hand or a foot. Each child is learning about keeping safe "in their own body".

'There are nettles close to the side of a path; the children walk through this path with their hands above their heads. When they arrive, some of them put a piece of dock leaf in their pocket, just in case; and often they share it with others when they get stung.'

A deep respect for the natural world

All three leaders have been trained in an approach called Forest School, which encourages hands-on learning through regular outdoor activities, usually in woodland, although Cowgate Under Fives Centre uses Johnston Terrace because they believe it's important for the children to appreciate, and feel ownership of a local wild place.

They observe that the children are more likely to care for nature. Jane: 'Such a small place of nature becomes like the world. Everything becomes really precious. One child was scared of bees and by observing the bees among the flowers, we were able to explain that we're all here for a reason. I do think that the children learn a deep respect of the natural world.'

As they talk of this very urban place of nature, they give the feeling that humans are visitors and that this secret garden is first and foremost the home of the insects, birds and frogs. As Teresa says: 'It's a space that's imbued with feeling. We are very conscious that we are creating memories that may well last a whole lifetime.'

Green potential: the Patrick Geddes Gardening Club

Catriona Grant has family connections with the Old Town that go back to her great-great-grandfather, who came over from Ireland in the 1850s and settled in James Court. But today, her eye is on the future, not the past: in particular, the potential she sees for vibrant green spaces in the Old Town.

For a start, Catriona's Canongate flat has a large tarmacked backgreen where she grows herbs in pots and tatties in bags. 'Few people use our backgreen, except maybe local restaurant staff for a ciggie. I'm one of the very few people who hangs out washing yet we've got 25 washing poles! Backgreens are so often quite literally a waste of space, a neglected eyesore, yet in terms of greening the Old Town they are potentially the jewel in the crown.' (Backgreens, the shared open space behind most tenements, make up more than half of Edinburgh's potential green space. According to the Edinburgh Community Backgreens Association, more than half of Edinburgh's population live in tenements - the proportion is considerably higher in the Old Town - and most tenements have a backgreen.)

But Catriona sees even wider potential: 'There's a multitude of gap sites, like the very large one on New Street, and many more that are smaller, and almost forgotten. There are dozens of underused little nooks and crannies like the little courtyard off Tweeddale Close. There's roof gardens and potential roof gardens. Oh, and did I mention Greyfriars and Canongate graveyards? In the Old Town, there is so much potential green space, it hardly seems urban!'

Hands in the soil

Catriona is Convener of the Patrick Geddes Gardening Club. The Club is actually a project of the Old Town Development Trust, which was set up by local residents in 2009 to encourage community-led development in the Old Town. Membership of the Club is open to anyone interested in gardening in the Old Town. At the Club's heart are residents who want to garden, but have little access to land as things stand: 'If you want to garden in the Old Town, the only way is collectively.' With a groundswell of interest behind the Club, a core of six to ten people attend monthly meetings, but Catriona says there are at least fifty more people who are keen to get their hands in the soil.

'We're discussing quite a few projects, some small and some quite grand.' 'Small' might include what Catriona calls 'Geddes gardening' rather than guerrilla gardening, with a few group members bringing along trowels and seeds to cheer up small spaces with a few colourful plants. More ambitiously, the Club has been given permission to garden in existing beds in Canongate Kirkyard, where [in July 2011], they have planted a variety of herbs and bedding plants, with plans for full herb beds and possibly a couple of Victoria plum trees.

The biggest project is a secluded courtyard garden behind Acheson House, a 17th century Canongate townhouse which belongs to Edinburgh Council. Having lain empty for twenty years, the building is about to take on new life as the offices of Edinburgh World Heritage Trust (EWHT). Both Edinburgh Council and EWHT are supporting the Geddes Gardening Club and gardening classes are about to begin. Currently a riot of weeds and overgrown trees, a group has met to discuss a design, which will include some of the plants likely to have been grown in the original 17th century garden, but laid out for 21st century purposes as a peaceful space for gardening, socialising and relaxing, just a few yards from the Canongate.

A green future

Asked 'Where would you like to be in five years' time?', Catriona doesn't hesitate: 'For myself, I'd like to be a gardener. I'd like to see a network of gardens in the Old Town, windowboxes, roof gardens, courtyard and backgreen gardens growing food and flowers, and making space for beasties and animals too. I'd like the gardens to be our community halls, where we chat to our neighbours, where tourists and visitors can feel safe and where they can find out that the Old Town is more than just the Castle!'

Green shoots, Campbell's Close

Gardening and green spaces will show the Old Town in a new light: 'We're seen as a night-time economy, a tourist destination, not a community. If we have as many green and growing patches as we can, gardening claims our space. The community becomes visible to the many tourists and visitors who can see what we're doing. We're saying "Look, we're here!" but in a positive way.'

Does she see any significance in the Club's name? 'We agreed that calling it after Patrick Geddes gave us more legitimacy and vibrancy than calling it the Development Trust green space sub-committee! Grassroots gardening can be difficult. The Geddes Gardening Club moves us away from an individualistic notion of "This is my land". We're bound at some time to come up against authority: why can't we lift some paving stones and plant some flowers? Associating ourselves with Patrick Geddes legitimises what we are doing; we're the inheritors of some of his principles and values and thinking: we don't have to debate or reinvent them. Yet obviously we live in a different age, we don't need to copy his vision to the letter.

'The aim is for the Geddes Gardening Club not to be dependent on grants, even though these are really helpful to get things started. Our aim is the community doing it for themselves. Gardening links us into thinking about food, supermarkets, fair trade, climate change. The Old Town Development Trust is discussing establishing a food cooperative. Shopping is very expensive and difficult here. We've done a food survey of the sheltered housing complexes in the Old Town: older people who live in these want to be able to buy fresh food. So in five years' time, I'd like to see the Trust running a wee food market with herbs and vegetable boxes; learning about foraging; supporting small social enterprises, a baker, a micro brewery. It means not relying on supermarkets, and developing a better relationship with nature and food and space and one another.'

So Geddes's most famous phrase is also an inspiration: 'We really do "Think global, act local". The Old Town is a UNESCO World Heritage site, valued by people all over Scotland, and all over the world. It doesn't belong to us even though we live in it. We are custodians.'

Footnotes

[1] Tess Darwin: *The Scots Herbal: the plant lore of Scotland*, Mercat Press, 1996

[2] Held in the Edinburgh and Scottish Collection, City of Edinburgh Public Library

[3] Most of the information on the planting is from *Dunbar's Close Garden Plant List*, a leaflet by Anna Buxton.

[4] Dennison, E. Patricia: *Holyrood and Canongate: a thousand years of history*; Birlinn, 2005

[5] Forbes W Robertson: *Early Scottish Gardeners and their Plants 1650 - 1750*; Tuckwell Press, 2000

[6] www.education.ed.ac.uk

[7] The information on gardeners and plants in this section has been gathered from *Early Scottish Gardeners* with kind permission from Professor Robertson.

[8] Darwin: *The Scots Herbal*

[9] D. Doyle: *Edinburgh Doctors and their Physic Gardens*, Edinburgh College of Physicians, Journal 38 -4 2008; www.rcpe.org.uk

[10] Jane Corrie, in her Greenyonder Tour, 'Hidden History' identifies seven.

[11] Robertson, *Early Scottish gardeners*

[12] Jim Johnson and Lou Rosenburg: *Renewing Old Edinburgh: the enduring legacy of Patrick Geddes*, Argyll Publishing, 2010

[13] D. Bell: *Edinburgh Old Town: the forgotten nature of an urban form*, Tholis Publishing, 2008

[14] The title of this section is from an Outlook Tower leaflet, 1926, held in the Edinburgh and Scottish Collection, City of Edinburgh Public Library

[15] Lileen Hardy: *The Diary of a Free Kindergarten*, Gay and Hancock, 1912

[16] Johnston and Rosenberg: *Renewing Old Edinburgh*

[17] www.camera-obscura.co.uk

[18] From an untitled press cutting in a folder retrieved from the Outlook Tower, now avaiable in Strathcyde University Library

[19] Hardy: *Diary of a Free Kindergarten*

Select Bibliography

Tess Darwin *The Scots Herbal: the plant lore of Scotland*, Mercat Press, 1996

E Patricia Dennison *Holyrood and Canongate: a thousand years of history*, Birrlinn, 2005

D. Doyle *Edinburgh Doctors and their Physic Gardens*, Edinburgh College of Physicians, Journal 38 -4 2008; www.rcpe.org.uk

Lileen Hardy *The Diary of a Free Kindergarten*, Gay and Hancock, 1912

Jim Johnson and Lou Rosenburg *Renewing Old Edinburgh: the enduring legacy of Patrick Geddes*, Argyll Publishing, 2010

Forbes W Robertson *Early Scottish Gardeners and their Plants 1650 - 1750*, Tuckwell Press, 2000

Patrick Geddes

Strathclyde University Library holds a large archive on Patrick Geddes and the Outlook Tower, including original photographs and lantern slides.

The Edinburgh and Scottish Collection in the City of Edinburgh Public Library holds a small number of pamphlets from the Outlook Tower.

The Patrick Geddes Trust website is an excellent source of information, and suggests further reading. www.patrickgeddestrust.co.uk

Moray House

The University of Edinburgh website includes a history of the original 17th century house and garden. www.ed.ac.uk Follow the links to 'Moray House' then 'History'.

Acknowledgements

First and foremost, my thanks to Royal Mile gardeners who have made the gardens and welcomed me into them: Anja Amsel, Eric Drake, Neil Ross and Fenella Kerr of Chessels Court for sharing coffee, personal research, and a pear from Miss Hardy's tree; Yvonne Farquhar, Faye Sweeney and Anne Jones of Coinyie House Close; Liz Edwards and all the residents of Fountain Court; Myer Lacome of Campbell's Close; Sylvia von Hartmann of White Horse Close; Anna Buxton and David Lownie, Dunbar's Close Garden; Jocelyn Lockhart, Grassmarket Community Project. Johnston Terrace Wildlife Garden: thanks to all who keep that wee wild space alive, especially Julian Warman of Scottish Wildlife Trust and Donna Begg, Teresa Bolger and Jane Garven of Cowgate Under Fives Centre. To all in the Patrick Geddes Gardening Club, especially Catriona Grant, Wendy Hebard, Jean Alexander and Janet Dick. The ambition to green the Old Town is inspiring: more power to your spades!

Big thanks to my fellow Greenyonder tour guides: Jane Corrie, who has given me great support and friendship since the beginning of Greenyonder Tours, and who introduced me to Edinburgh's physic gardens; and Julia Cook who has inspired me with her knowledge and passion for healing plants, which she conveys to others like no-one else I know. To Ben Young and Lesley Roberts for thorough proof reading.

I am very grateful to Professor Forbes W Robertson for permission to quote quite extensively from his enjoyable and informative book *Early Scottish Gardeners and their Plants 1650 - 1750*. The staff at Strathclyde University Archives were very supportive during my research there into the Patrick Geddes gardens. Peder Aspen, archivist of Old Saint Paul's Church shared his knowledge of Lileen Hardy and Saint Saviours Child Garden Nursery.

A few organisations of interest

City of Edinburgh Council supports Old Town gardens in a variety of ways, both as a local authority and through individual staff.

Edinburgh Community Backgreens Association supports tenement dwellers to work with their neighbours to create beautiful and productive backgreens. www.ecba.org.uk

Edinburgh Old Town Association works on behalf of those who live and work in the Old Town of Edinburgh to influence the way the area is developed and to improve the environment and quality of life. www.eota.org.uk

Edinburgh World Heritage is a charity with the role of conserving, protecting and promoting the city's World Heritage Site, which covers both the Old and New Towns. EWH has supported several Old Town gardens. www.ewht.org.uk

Grassmarket Community Project works with adults who are marginalised for a variety of reasons, with an emphasis on skills training and social enterprise, such as making furniture using recycled pews, a 'Plough to Plate' food programme and café, a textile making project', and gardening in Greyfriars Kirkyard. www.grassmarketcommunityproject.co.uk

Patrick Geddes Gardening Club is a project of the Old Town Development Trust and meets regularly to garden in several plots and to take forward initiatives around green space. Membership is open to anyone interested in gardening and growing things in the Old Town. www.eotdt.org / email geddesgardeningclub@yahoo.co.uk

Scottish Wildlife Trust is dedicated to the protection of all of Scotland's wildlife, raises public awareness of threatened habitats and species and manages 123 reserves Scotland-wide, of which Johnston Terrace is the smallest and most urban. www.swt.org.uk

Picture credits

p84 'Little gardeners'. Photograph by Francis C. Inglis, Calton Hill, Edinburgh, showing nursery children working in the garden of St Saviour's, originally published in *Diary of a Free Kindergarten* by Lileen Hardy, 1912. Reproduced by permission of Edinburgh City Libraries.

p89 'Norah Geddes's sketch plan for King's Wall Garden', from an unpublished folder of sketch plans and drawings, entitled 'Edinburgh Open Spaces, carried out at one time or another, (N.G.Mears)', 1909 - 1914. Reproduced by permission of University of Strathclyde Library, Department of Archives and Special Collections.

p98 'Litter picking in Johnston Terrace Wildlife Garden'. © Jane Garven

All other photographs © Jean Bareham

www.greenyondertours.com

The Rothiemay map, 1647

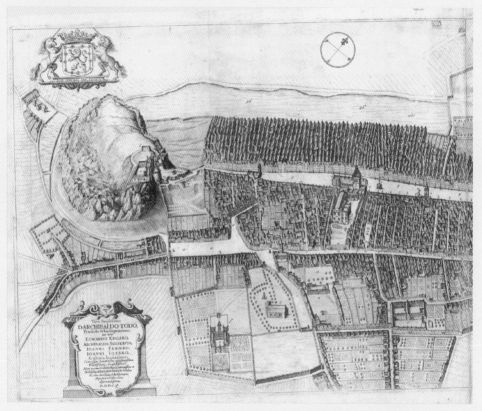